MY MALAWI JOURNAL

Bea Buckley

ATHENA PRESS
LONDON

ISBN 1 931456 48 8

First Published 2003 by
ATHENA PRESS
Queen's House, 2 Holly Road
Twickenham TW1 4EG
United Kingdom

Printed for Athena Press

MY MALAWI JOURNAL

Preface

"Where in the world is Malawi?"

"You're going to Maui? How lucky can you get?"

"I told someone you were going to Mali. I've never heard of Malawi."

Typical of the questions and comments I heard from friends, relatives, etc., when I told them I was going to Malawi, or they had heard I was going and were curious.

Yes. Malawi. M-A-L-A-W-I..." I felt I was running a continuous tape of repetition as I explained all I knew, which wasn't much, about the country that had invited me to be a Peace Corps Volunteer. One person I met before I left knew where it was.

As I was making preparations to leave, I went to the J.C. Penny outlet at the Franklin Park Mall. I wanted a fresh battery for my watch; a Timex that only ticks when it has a working battery. I also have a wind-up number that I have had for many years. It ticks when I wind it. I only use it during a power outage. I was planning to take it also; however, this is only peripherally pertinent to the fact that I met someone who knew where Malawi was located.

The lady was in the watch repair department. When I explained I wanted a fresh battery for my watch, I jokingly told her I wanted one with a two-year guarantee as I was leaving the country for that long. Please note how I wanted to let someone know I had received an invitation to a country...

She, being a sales person, took my bait and asked, "Where are you going?"

When I told her, "Malawi," she did not say, "Where is that?"

She said, "Oh, yes. East central Africa."

Someone knew where Malawi was! I wasn't leaving to drop off the face of the earth! It was really a country, not just a government plot to do away with do-gooder old folks. Wow! One thing bothered me about this. The lady was not a product of the

American educational system. She spoke flawless English with a German accent. Oh, well...

I learned a lot about Malawi, starting with the information sent me by the Peace Corps Malawi Office. It was all interesting; reality was more so, as I discovered, bit by bit and day by day.

Malawi is a small, landlocked country in east central Africa. If you look at your globe or world map, locate thirty degrees longitude east of Greenwich where it crosses ten degrees latitude south of the Equator, slide your finger a little south-east, it should rest on Malawi, or close. A guess would be thirty-five degrees longitude, fifteen degrees latitude. The country is surrounded by Tanzania on the north, north-east, Mozambique, east and south and Zambia on the west. It has been compared in size to the state of Pennsylvania; area, not shape. Pennsylvania weighs in at 45,316 square miles and Malawi at 45,747. Malawi is about five hundred twenty miles long, north-south and anywhere from five to one hundred miles wide, east-west. About sixty percent of the eastern border is composed of Lake Malawi; a border shared with Mozambique. The lake is about three hundred fifty miles long and perhaps sixty miles at its widest point. Malawi claims sovereignty over most of the lake, including some islands near the Mozambique border.

Lake Malawi is Africa's third largest lake, Lake Victoria being the largest and Lake Tanganyika second in size. The lake was formed in the Great Rift which reaches from the Red Sea southward. This is otherwise known as a fault in the earth's crust.

This caused a little concern for me one day when I was sick, all by myself in the house, lying in bed, feeling sorry for myself. The bed started to move, the walls were moving, things hanging on hooks swinging! I thought, This is not a hypnagogic hallucination! This is an earthquake! And I remembered reading about the lake forming in the Great Rift... I wondered what thoughts conjured in the minds of Californians, who live their lives on one of those things (a fault), when the ground begins to move under them? No one else seemed remotely concerned at the time; the young folks continued about their business in the backyard. If that had happened in Toledo, it would have been on the six o'clock news. Oh, well. To paraphrase Peter Beagle, "It was either an act of God or it wasn't. In any case nothing could be done about it."

Back to the lake. Lake Malawi reaches depths of more than two thousand feet and is fifteen hundred feet, give or take a few, above sea level. It is fed by approximately fourteen rivers and drained by one, the Shire. Unfortunately for me and also a great disappointment, I didn't get to see the lake during my too short stay in Malawi. Anything I can tell about the lake came from word of mouth, class or books and encyclopedias.

It, the lake, does support commercial fishing and is reported to have more than two hundred varieties of fish. No fish are able to survive in the lower depths of the lake due to lack of oxygen and the presence of hydrogen sulfide in concentrations too great to support life.

Although in some areas along the lake the land may rise two thousand or more feet, there are beaches where swimming is safe. I understand it is the only lake in east Africa that is not completely contaminated with the snails that carry the parasitic fluke responsible for schistosomiasis.

Schistosomiasis is one of those unpronounceable diseases on the Red Cross blood donor questionnaire that is filled out each time someone donates blood. Old time, frequent donors don't think too much about the question as they know their blood is good, they know the rules and the Red Cross loves them for it. But first time donors are sometimes surprised that the Red Cross wants clean, healthy blood.

"Have you ever had schistosomiasis?"

"Oh, my God!"

"What's that?"

"How would I know if I had it?"

They would know if they had it. An earlier question about having been out of the country within a specified time frame would be a clue. The disease is common in countries where sanitary conditions are not pristine. It is caused by a parasitic fluke with a life cycle that includes water, snails and an animal or human host. So, if you don't want to get schistosomiasis, you don't drink or go swimming in snail water.

When doing a life cycle, one could start anywhere, since it is a cycle but I guess the egg would be the logical place to start, assuming an adult produced the egg. The eggs are in the urine and feces of an infected animal or person. Gross as it seems, in some areas where animals are not kept away from water sources, they walk into the water to drink and often urinate and defecate in same said water. If the animal happens to be infected with the fluke, the stool and urine will contain eggs. The whole mess falls into the water wherein live the snails.

Snails are not very high on the food chain and scavenge around in the murky depths, eating whatever comes their way. Animal excreta is as much a banquet to them as a filet mignon would be to us. People keep snails in fish tanks as they clean up the fish excreta. But anyway, here is this snail dining on excreta containing fluke eggs.

The eggs hatch into larvae, which the snails deposit into the water. Now, we have all these little larvae swimming around in the water just waiting for a poor innocent, unsuspecting animal or human to take a drink, go swimming, wading or whatever. They can and do go through the skin and into the bloodstream. Here they set up housekeeping; actually they grow into adults first, before they set up housekeeping and produce eggs. Typical of adolescents, they raise all sorts of havoc while growing to adulthood, eating the food and drinking the blood of their poor victim as well as other disgusting things.

The end result of this behavior is eggs in the urine and feces of the host. This may, just may, be deposited in water for the always hungry snails, continuing the cycle. The hapless host becomes anemic, passes blood in his, or her, urine and stools and becomes generally run down and poorly. The moral of this is, one really should be careful about what one eats or drinks and where one deposits bodily waste. There are all sorts of critters whose sole purpose is to eat stuff and turn it into something else. Woe be unto you if you get caught in the life cycle of one of these!

Lake Malawi still has beaches where swimming is safe and they do check for the presence of the snails. The rivers, streams and other water sources are not necessarily safe.

I think I started this to give an idea about the place where I was; I get sidetracked easily. Probably the best source of information about Malawi is in books already written and waiting in the library. I found some great books, aimed for young readers, that were informative and easy reading.

For all Malawi's small size and lack of news coverage, it has a long and interesting history. The lake apparently attracted ancient people as human fossils have been found dating back many thousands of years.

The area has been populated by different tribes, one being overpowered by the next. It was a major source of slaves for the Arab and Portuguese slave traders. David Livingston, an explorer-missionary, was the first European to see the lake and given credit for naming it "Lake Nyasa", "Nyasa" being a native word for "lake". Thus he named it "Lake-lake". The land around it he named "Nyasaland" or "Lakeland".

Livingston was distressed about the slave trade that was going on as were the other missionaries to the area. They began a movement in England to stop the activity in the area. The British successfully stopped the slave trade and Nyasaland became part of the British colonial empire.

Nyasaland remained part of the British Empire until the early sixties when it became independent. It was governed by a Congress and a president, Hastings Banda. Banda was essentially a dictator until his loss of an election in 1994. Bakili Muluzi is now the president. This paragraph leaves out much interesting, to me, information. If it interests you also, there are many good sources of information. I did not plan to write a never-ending thesis; only my journal for friends and family.

I spent the time I was there in the Central District which is mostly plateau; this with an elevation of twenty-five hundred to forty-five hundred feet. I had read all this information before I left but couldn't remember the elevation here. No wonder I was out of breath on the mountain!

I hope you enjoy my journal.

Day I

Wednesday, April 17, 1996

Toledo Express seemed moderately busy but that was the last thing on my mind. As I stood in line waiting to check in my two large bags, I had to force myself to keep my thoughts on the business at hand. My backpack was heavy. I carried it with one strap over my right shoulder. The two large bags I pushed along the smooth floor with my foot as the line inched its way to the counter. The bags, of the proper specified dimensions, had little wheels. This made moving them easier than handling the backpack. The bags were all overweight. I was hoping they wouldn't be too picky. I didn't need to worry about the weight here, but wasn't too sure what to expect on the overseas flight.

The large bags each weighed about forty-one or forty-two pounds. Lifting each one alone was no big deal. With a twenty plus pound backpack on my shoulders... Well, I'm an old lady. Richard had carried the large bags from his Bronco to the check-in line. He had to move the car from the drop-off area to the parking lot. I must deal with this myself; keep pushing, Granny.

Checking the bags went quickly. The attendant neatly attached the destination tags, then handed me the folder with my tickets. Now I wouldn't need to worry about those bags until I arrived in Washington D.C.

Next through the scanner. I was rid of the backpack for the brief moment it took for it to ride through that. The backpack too was overweight. I wasn't sure what I was going to need or what I could live without for awhile. I thought it best to keep my little short wave radio, camera, and walkman with me. I didn't want to replace them before I arrived in Malawi. I'm sure I wouldn't after I got there.

Actually carrying the backpack wasn't much different than toting an overloaded purse. I have already carried purses in which

I had stuffed everything except the proverbial "kitchen sink". Besides the radio, etc., I had my books, *ODAT*, *Courage to Change*, and a paperback. The paperback I thought would keep my mind occupied in a pinch. It was one of a "classics" series. Cheap, three books in one by author Anthony Trollope. Heavy but lighter than three equivalent books, and extremely small print. Other than a few items of clothing, the rest of the stuff was of a heavy variety. Mary had given me the backpack as a going away gift. It is a large L.L. Bean number; now packed full.

Well, through the scanner and up the escalator with Kimberly, Jennifer and Richard in tow. Kimberly was skipping school and Jennifer left work to see me off. Richard also took time off work. He can set his own hours to a point, so that didn't count. He does put in long hours but is usually able to leave when necessary. I was grateful to have them there. I also appreciated Richard's wisecracks and running commentary. It helped to be reminded of the humorous aspect of things. Also it didn't give any of us the opportunity to start on the impending separation. I can handle this. One day at a time. I had my good cry yesterday, so if I keep my mind focused on the business at hand, I'll be okay.

The plane to Detroit X was a commuter number I think is part of Northwest Airlines. When it is time to leave, we wander to the east wing, a long hall, to the end. From a window we see a small red airplane that does not inspire confidence, waiting on the tarmac. Oh, well…

After hugs all around, I shoulder my backpack and go down a flight of stairs, out onto the tarmac, to the little red airplane. An attendant stopped me. He announced that there was no room under the seat for my backpack. I must put it on the luggage rack with everyone else's bags. No room for a backpack? Uh, oh!

Up the steps into what seems to be someone's toy airplane. I duck my head, walk down the aisle and find my seat, 7-A. I sit down, find my seat belt, fasten it, then look around. There is a single row of seats on either side of the narrow aisle. Nope, there is no room for a backpack under the seat. No room for it anywhere. I'm looking out the window and see a wing and a propeller. Well, God, if this is the way I am to go, so be it. You want me to lose my hearing? Well, I guess I accept that too. I may not like it, but I accept it.

The pilot is a good-looking young man. I just hope he is old enough to fly this thing. I have a problem with people looking so young. I remember, when I was forty, thinking how young the new doctors appeared. They certainly seemed older when I was in my twenties! Now I see people in their forties and wonder if I was ever that young.

Actually, it turns out the pilot is quite competent, the plane fairly quiet and also fast. That little red devil moved! Wow! Once we were allowed to take off, the flight was fun. I just had to relax and enjoy the ride. If the good Lord decides it is my time to meet him face to face, it will be a great way to go. Not much fun for the survivors but what the heck? Who asked them? Let's fly!

Getting to Detroit X didn't take long at all. Getting from point A to point B proved a little more complicated. I had to get the backpack from the luggage rack, then board a people mover to the terminal. The people mover had standing room only. I love people in crowds. It is as though there is no one else around. Each person is alone, surrounded on all sides by unacknowledged packages of poop. If you don't look at it, it doesn't exist. They also seem passively aggressive. To make matters worse, I'm carrying this oversized bag on my back. It is all I can do to get myself on the thing, let alone the baggage! I muscle my way onto the thing and ride in the crush to the terminal. One reason for my determination to get on that particular tram was an imperative need to visit the ladies room.

By the time I find a ladies room and wait in a never-ending line, I'm getting a wee bit weary of the backpack. Now I have it hooked over both shoulders to distribute the weight more evenly. When I get into a stall, there is another problem. Dealing with the backpack while I go through the maneuvers to empty my bladder. I manage to get it off my back without dropping it on the seat or into the water. It is so heavy, I am afraid it will break the hook on the door. I did manage to put it on the lower hook and push the hand grip close to the door so the downward pull would be closer to the door and less apt to break the hook from its mooring. See, I did learn something in high school physics class besides hating football, basketball, the guys who played them and the coaches worse. There isn't much room in those stalls and dealing with an unwieldy backpack didn't help. Put the pack on the floor? My beautiful, pristine L.L. Bean? Unthinkable! In retrospect laughable but at the time, unthinkable. I managed to do what I went there for and was ready for the next obstacle.

That would be washing my hands. Suzy Cool nonchalantly swung the strap over her shoulder and waited in the hand washing line. All was cool until the time came to bend over the sink, turn on the water and squirt soap on my hands. Thunk! The pack slid down my arm and almost knocked me into the poor soul at the next sink. I braced myself with the pack supported between the sink and my knee and washed my hands.

I managed to kill more time than I should have in the restroom. Now, down the concourse to the boarding area, get the ticket checked, and onto the plane. This was an *airplane*! No toy this time. My seat was 7-F. A window seat. This is nice. The third seat from the aisle. This is okay. There is a lady, at least I thought she was a lady, sitting in the middle seat. This is inconvenient. She did not acknowledge my, I thought, polite, "Excuse me?" It would have helped if she had moved her legs, even a little, or stood up to allow my passage; but she did not move or even look up. She probably thought I was the mad slasher and if she ignored me I would go slash someone else.

It was necessary for me to lift my backpack over her head and drop it on my seat. Then I had to step high over her lap without bumping her. Thank heaven I wasn't wearing heels and pantyhose. I managed my high step *sans incident*. The next project was to get the backpack off the seat, under the seat in front of mine and sit down. By some contortions I thought I was no longer capable of, I did all those things, sat down in my seat, fastened my seat belt and was glad to do so. The day isn't half over. Wow!

The flight was uneventful. The usual instructions about not smoking, what to do with the oxygen masks if they are needed, the exits, flotation devices, seat belt, etc. The little lady next to me is immobile. I exaggerate. She was probably just petrified to be flying and praying intently. I started reading *Barchester Towers* but didn't get a chance to read much. The flight was fast and to the point. We arrived at Washington National in short order.

Getting disembarked was much simpler than getting seated. My two seat mates – neither had luggage – were up and out with the first push. As soon as the seats were empty, I hoisted the backpack onto the aisle seat, waited for a break in the flow of humanity, stepped into the flow, became part of it and eventually arrived in the terminal.

The terminal was typical of large terminals. Flying, the actual flying, is a great way to travel. It is the rest of the folderol that makes one wish one had stayed home. Airports are miles from anywhere. Even Toledo X, which is a nice little airport, is twenty miles from town. Town is gradually moving to meet it, but it is still far out. The airports are similar to mini cities with streets going in all directions, shops, restaurants, you name it; it is at the airport of any major city.

By following the signs with arrows pointing to BAGGAGE CLAIM, I managed to find my way to the baggage carousel and the ground level. I don't know why waiting for luggage is such a trial. Yes, I do. There is always the chance the bags won't show up. You will stand there and wait and wait and wait. The carousel becomes empty and you are the only one with no bags! Or they go by and you don't recognize them! Both of mine arrive as they should, I snag them off and am ready to find a cab.

A gentleman (?), a fellow in a red hat, said, "You go out there to get a cab." He pointed to the street. At this point I had my backpack straps over both shoulders and one hand each on the handle of a large bag. Theoretically, I could pull them along on their little wheels and they would go where I went. Ready! Here we go! Let's get a cab!

The two large bags were not happy. They had just flown hundreds of miles in a dark cargo hold, packed in with just all sorts of other bags. They had been smashed, squashed, crushed, rudely thrown about and now they were rebelling. They were absolutely perverse. Wheeling right, then left, bumping into each other and people who were careless enough to get in the way of their rampages. It was a miracle we made it to the dispatcher at all.

This is a well-orchestrated procedure. A cab comes zooming up, the dispatcher points the next person in line to the cab, they get in, that cab leaves, the next cab rolls up, etc. There are two traffic lanes of boarding cabs. Smooth operation. Young business types in dark suits, white shirts, power ties and a briefcase get the cabs at the curb. The old, gray-haired lady in jeans, sweatshirt, sneakers, backpack and two unwieldy rolly bags gets the cab in the street!

Hey! I lucked out with the cab driver. He threw the unpleasant bags in the trunk and slammed the lid. Then he assisted me and my still pristine backpack into the cab and whisked us away to the Four H Center, 7100 Connecticut Ave., Chevy Chase, Maryland. He knew where he was going. He let me out in front of the center building, took the bags out of the trunk, deposited them in the driveway, I paid him and he was gone.

Here I am, standing in front of a large wood frame building with several doors and dealing with one hundred pounds plus of luggage. Some of it is on wheels but I was going to have to lift it up some steps. There was no doorman nor bellhop so it was up to me. Come on, Granny! You're going to spend the next two years in the Peace Corps! You can do this! Let's go!

The only person in sight is a petite woman. One of those second-class citizens, denied their rights by the militants, forced to stand out of doors to enjoy a cigarette. She has short curly red hair of a shade that comes from a bottle. Probably younger than she looks. She does look harmless enough, just a little care worn. Regardless of what the politically correct police say, I find smokers are generally pleasant, thoughtful, humane people. As long as they have the drug of their choice.

I approached her after lifting the big bags up the two or three steps to the front "porch" of this oversized farmhouse. I explained why I was here, and could she direct me to where I belonged? She didn't say it but I suspect from her body language that she wanted to direct me straight to the fiery furnace and the man with the horns and tail. I'm sorry; there is no brass band, welcoming committee, balloons or even someone with a label announcing, "Hello! I am—" How am I to know? She did point to the center door and mention there was a receptionist's desk there. That would have been my first guess. However, with all the luggage, I didn't want to haul it all in there and be told to move it someplace else. There were other buildings at right angles to this one.

Pulling the fairly subdued bags behind me, I headed for the center door, opened it, lifted the bags through one at a time and placed them on the floor inside. Sure enough! There was a desk with a receptionist! Continuing my trek from the door to the desk with the twenty plus pound backpack on my shoulders and dragging the recalcitrant bags, I faced the receptionist. After telling her my story, she said, "Yes. You are at the right place." My room was No. 3206. She handed me a plastic card and pointed to the elevator.

My room was on the second floor not the thirty-second as the number would indicate. To this day, I have no idea what the three indicated. Probably just some government bureaucrats at work. I thanked the lady who was doing some important work at her desk. She didn't acknowledge me any further so I turned and dragged my burdens to the elevator. I pushed the up button and waited. Nothing happened. I pushed the button again. Still nothing.

Just about this time who should appear but a lovely, young, bubbly girl with flaming red hair. This red hair was the real Mc Coy. That color doesn't come from a bottle. She was carrying her bags. Guess what? The elevator doesn't work and we must use the stairs. Would she show me the stairway? Oh, sure. Follow me. She had already learned the ropes and her way around. I love these generation Xers. They are so clever and quick!

Her name was Barbara. She showed me the stairs, how to get to my room, helped me open the door. Using the card in that door was tricky. She went on to her room. I dropped my back-pack on the floor, closed the door and went back downstairs to get one of the large bags. I was glad I wasn't on the thirty-second floor! With some practice I managed to unlock the door with the plastic card. The bag was dumped on the floor next to the backpack, the door closed and I was on my way to fetch the last bag. I hauled that one up the stairs and to my door.

Hoo! Hoo! The card wouldn't work. I tried this. I tried that. Nothing. I couldn't get the door open. Now what?

Who should appear but my little angel of mercy, Barbara. She tried the card with no better luck than I. No problem. Put the bag in her room and deal with it later. Good idea. We did it. Then went downstairs for registration.

Wow! I walked into a large room where there was a frenzy of activity. Who should introduce himself but "Woody". I knew Woody. He was the voice on the phone of the Malawi desk in Washington. Now here he was in person. I had spoken to him often. I knew someone. What a relief! It wasn't totally unknown.

I soon met more people, other Peace Corps trainees (P.C.T.s); same as me. And the Peace Corps staff.

One lady, Joanne, seemed to be in charge of all the details. There were insurance papers to sign. My passport needed to be signed but Joanne kept that. The passports of all the P.C.T.s had to stay together. I guess keeping track of twenty-three people about to be sent overseas requires much in the way of organizational skills. She appeared to have it all together. I was reassured. I was given back my birth certificate and also given money for expenses.

Some of the staff were former Peace Corps volunteers who had served in Malawi. There was a good ratio of staff to trainees. We did some "get acquainted" stuff such as all of us sitting around a large table and telling something about ourselves.

I'm trying to remember exactly what I said. Something to the effect that I was a retired nurse with grown-up children and grandchildren who really didn't need me and could get along fine without me. All perfectly true. The strange thing, to me, was that most of those around me seemed to think it was sad. That none of my family needed me. Actually, I think it is something to be happy about. Perhaps the way I said it came across as poignant. I didn't mean it that way. My children love me as I love them. However, they aren't dependent upon me and haven't been for a long time. Plus they all seem to be doing a creditable job of parenting my grandchildren. I'm going to miss them all. Probably a lot if I allow myself to think about it. I am responsible for my thoughts, attitude and actions. If I choose not to dwell on sad things to the point of having a major pity party, there shouldn't be a problem.

There is no reason why I shouldn't do something I have wanted to do for a long time at this point in my life. I'm not getting any younger. If I look for an excuse not to do something,

I'll find one. I certainly will be a more interesting grandparent to my grandchildren if I can write to them and tell them of a world that will only widen their awareness.

I am the oldest person in this group. And the only nurse. There are quite a few child survival officers and HIV counselors. The education seems to be social work, occupational therapy, physical therapy, teaching and psychology. One has a degree in public health. The rest of the group seem to be agriculture specialists. I can't remember names yet. No one in the group looks over thirty. I imagine some may be, but judging by looks and actions, thirty is tops. They act younger, but as they are unmarried, that can carry on into the thirties. Marriage and children seems to mellow and stabilize most people. I have known people who married young and started families who acted older than their appearance would indicate. Just plain responsibility does it too. Actually, in this society it is easier to judge a person's age by their actions than appearance. I'll probably find out later how old everyone is. It doesn't really make any difference except I wonder if I'll be able to keep up...

We were issued meal tickets to have punched each time we use them. The cafeteria and dining room are in another building, the Kellogg Building. I wonder if it was endowed by the cereal people. The building is to the left as you walk out the front door of this building. It sits at right angles to this one and is nearest the street, Connecticut Avenue.

After the scheduled program, speeches, etc., we were allowed to get our evening meal. The dining room was large, loud and confusing. The food was uninspiring, palatable and filling. I've eaten better. I've eaten worse. Some of my own cooking in both instances. I couldn't find anyone around who wanted to punch my meal ticket. If they don't care, I don't. I ate, then went to check the place out.

I met my room-mate. She is young (what else?), attractive, with a sweet smile, long dark hair, petite, Irish and her name is Cathy. There are just two of us assigned to the room although there are two metal bunk beds, one on either side of the room, giving the room a capacity of four. It reminded me of my introduction to St. Luke's Hospital School of Nursing, circa 1950.

The senior class hadn't been sent away on affiliation yet and they had no place to put several of us. Five of us were assigned to a classroom in the basement of the nurses' home. There we stayed for several weeks. We slept in hospital beds; the old high from the floor numbers. We didn't mind. We had a weeks-long slumber party! We are still good friends. Four of us, anyway. One of the group finished the three years, disappeared and was never heard from again. I revise that statement. No one we know has heard from her since. The rest of us have lunch together once a month and discuss children, grandchildren and life's adventures. I'm going to miss that. They all think I am nuts; but do remember, I had at one point planned to be a missionary. In retrospect, I wouldn't have been a good one. Besides, considering the time frame, I probably would have been eaten by the Mau-Mau.

Back to my room. There was the obligatory desk, chairs, lamps, etc. We each chose a bottom bunk. I am on the right, entering the room and Cathy on the left. Cathy is from Philadelphia, had friends and plans so other than routine pleasantries we each pretty much did our thing.

I probably could have joined some young people and done some wild and interesting things. However, at this point I need to sit down and contemplate the day's activities and the game plan for the next few days. There won't be a dull moment, I'm afraid.

My first evening consisted of checking out the bathroom, brushing my teeth, etc., digging a nightshirt out of a bag and reading until my eyes closed.

Day II

Thursday, April 18, 1996

I woke up early, dug some clothes out of my bag, snagged up the soap, wash cloth, shampoo, towel, etc., and trudged down the hall to the bathroom, did the morning routine, shower, teeth, etc. I just had my hair cut so it is short, will dry quickly and stay fairly tidy. I'm wondering where I'll get it cut again. It should be okay for six weeks but I won't be through training by then. So I look like a wild woman. Can't worry about it – low priority. I'll cross that bridge when I come to it.

No one was in the bathroom, a community affair, while I was there. However, several of the others were already at breakfast when I got to the dining room. More uninspired food. What did I expect? If I were at home, I would be eating cold cereal or toast and decaf. This morning a gentleman was in attendance and my meal ticket was punched. I had more to eat last evening without having it punched! So there!

It is a beautiful spring day; sunshine, fluffy white clouds in a blue sky, trees in bloom, trees with tiny new leaves, flowers in colorful array! Wow! Washington must be just enough south that spring is here already. It was cold when I left Toledo X and has been. Not spring-like back there at all.

Today is health day. Two nurses from Medical Services came to talk to us about our health. I should never get sick with all the immunizations I'll be getting!

A bus was supposed to come, pick us up and deliver us to the Hubert Humphrey Building. This is where we get our first shots; MMR, IVP, and yellow fever vaccine. We waited patiently until long past the appointed time. The nurses had co-ordinated this but somehow there was a foul-up.

Someone called for cabs (it was probably Joanne). Then we had to wait longer for them to arrive. We continued to mill aimlessly around until the cabs started to show up. Everyone was anxious to get to the destination. I' m not sure why. I'll put off getting a shot as long as I can. The cabs quickly filled with four riders each and drove off. Finally, one nurse, Carol, and three trainees were left. I was one of the last group. We three trainees climbed into the back seat and Carol rode shotgun.

Hoorah! We are off on our Washington adventure!

Our cab driver appeared to me to be either Pakistani or of east Indian nationality. As he talked to Carol, we discover he is Ethiopian and had only been driving a cab for five days! He was quite interesting; he was an historian, was writing a book, had been a student of Senator Paul Tsongas when the senator was in the Peace Corps many years ago and spoke excellent English. Unfortunately, as he had only been driving the cab for five days, he was not familiar with D.C.

So… we have a cabbie who knows a lot, but not how to get around the nation's capital. The Hubert Humphrey Building is located at 200 SW Independence Ave. We drove by it, unknown to us, and on to 200 SE Independence Ave. When it was obvious that was not the correct destination, he turned around, retraced our route and at long last deposited us at the Humphrey Building. That ride cost us twenty-eight dollars. We are to be reimbursed for that; our tax dollars at work!

The Humphrey Building, another example of our tax dollars, was not a particularly beautiful building. I was rather expecting something more substantial appearing. I'm not a Democrat, but I liked and admired Mr. Humphrey and was disappointed in the building bearing his name. I'm sure there are those who are more knowledgeable than me, who think it is the greatest example of architecture of the twentieth century. I know what I like and that wasn't it.

We were the last of the groups to arrive and everyone else was already in the nurses' lair where we were to get our shots. The security people were not much help but we managed to find the place in spite of them. Then we had to wait our turns. It was decided I didn't need the MMR. The general consensus was, if I had reached my advanced age without catching any of those diseases, I was immune so the shot was unnecessary. I'll buy that.

I did however, get the IVP and yellow fever numbers. All this took time; what with the paper shuffling, waiting our turn, waiting to be sure we didn't go into anaphylactic shock, the time passed. Oh, yes. We were issued Mefloquine tablets. "Take one now and one each week for the duration of the stay in Malawi." They issued a goodly supply; also a paper listing the side effects, etc. These were fairly routine. I read it and put it somewhere, never to be seen again. I think I left it there as I can't find it.

After we finished with the immunizations, eight of us walked to the Union Station. This was not far. We walked through the Capitol grounds which are beautiful. I enjoyed that immensely. The idea was to have lunch at one of the restaurants in the Union Station. We chose the American. Here we were all seated around a large round table. There was a great variety of foods to pick from the menu. I chose to have a hamburger and a Diet Pepsi. Not very original but I'm a fairly ordinary person and I happen to like hamburgers. I think I was the only person at the table who ordered one. Am I being defensive about this? Perhaps. My hamburger was large and filling!

Next we headed for the Metro so we could take that to Friendship Heights. I was following the others as they seemed to know where they were going and I didn't. There are a lot of people rushing thither and yon down underground. I was afraid I would lose the others as they were speeding through the place. Our group had divided after lunch and I chose to go with the Metro group which was the speedy one! I didn't lose them and managed to get on the train. Once on the train the ride was uneventful. Traveling very fast between stations, people getting on, people getting off, etc. Nothing to look at out the window except expanses of concrete at the stops. Finally, Friendship Heights!

We get off the Metro and try to find a cab. That takes a little time, but we get one. The driver "thought" we told him Wisconsin Ave. instead of Connecticut Ave. and took us to 7100 Wisconsin Ave. Wrong! Meanwhile the meter is ticking away! I wonder if some of these fellows do that just to get money from unsuspecting tourists. The cab fare was way high but he let us get away with ten dollars because of "his" mistake. I can't believe cab drivers don't know their way around the place. I lucked out with the cab driver I had yesterday from the airport. Today, I'm glad I had to walk into the street to get the driver I had! Two lost cabbies in one day?

We made it back in time for our one thirty class. Now the indoctrination begins in earnest. Getting along with others, being able to work with others, getting around in a strange country; they kept us busy. It was interesting but my cup runneth over and spilleth all over the place. I have no mental capacity to learn more at this point!

By dinner time I was maxed out and headed for my room. For some crazy reason I looked at the expiration date on my Mefloquine tablets in the process of putting them away. Ha! Expired! I don't feel like dealing with this now. I'll mention it to the powers that be later. I'll be in Malawi when I take the next one. Tomorrow I'll go to the gift shop to see if they have postcards and laundry soap. I'll need to wash clothes before leaving. I don't want to pack dirty clothing. No! No! No!

Day III

Friday, April 19, 1996

What a day! More indoctrination! The Returned Peace Corps Volunteers (R.P.C.V.) who are helping with our orientation are pretty neat. They put on some skits for us that were fun. One involved traveling by bus. They had trainees in this one – as passengers. It was a riot! I've been there. Done that.

No animals on the buses or trains, but I sure remember the crowding. When they still had good bus and train services, in the forties and fifties, the buses and trains were often filled beyond capacity. I remember one trip when I was in training. I had to stand the whole trip from Port Clinton to Toledo with my suitcase between my feet. There was no place to put it. It was so crowded I couldn't even sit on it.

The city buses were as bad during rush hours. When I was eight months pregnant with Richard, I had to take a bus downtown to see the doctor. Richard was born in July and it was as hot in June as it can only get hot around bricks and pavement. No air conditioning on the buses either. Going for the appointment was not too bad; coming home was another story! The men from offices were going home, the shoppers were going home, the tired store clerks and secretaries were on their way home and so was I. This trip was the pits except for one dear lady of mature age. The bus was filled to the front with standers. Men were no more chivalrous in 1953 than they are now. It was an elderly lady who stood up and insisted I sit down! Back to the buses! At least I'm not pregnant!

We were told of some customs that are different from ours and we would be expected to observe while in the villages. No public affection between members of the opposite sex. Handholding between same sex persons is the norm although homosexuality is *verboten*. No shorts or slacks for the ladies.

Neither sex exposes any area between the waist and the knees in public. Knees are naughty.

We had pizza for lunch. Pizza is always fun to eat. It was a big hit with everyone. These were quite good, at least the two pieces I sampled were. There were several varieties; combinations of toppings. No way could I sample them all.

After lunch we had a two-hour break. I thought I could use that time to get my laundry detergent and postcards. I went through the game room to the gift shop. The proprietress was not there! She was on her lunch break. She would be back at one thirty. I had to be back in class at two. I read until one thirty, went back to the gift shop, bought the postcards and detergent, then back to my room. I managed to address half the postcards before class...

There is a sunny patio behind the main or center building. We went out there for part of our sessions. Mostly talk. We had one where we wrote something about ourselves. The papers were hung up around the gazebo and we walked around and read each one. It was an interesting exercise. I am impressed with the lives and experiences of my fellow trainees.

Going outdoors for classes was a pleasant break. I'm finding my way around the cafeteria now, but we are on our own tonight. I hit the vending machines in the game room. I love vending machines and had a field day "junking it".

Around seven in the evening I took my dirty laundry to the McCormick Building. This building is next to the Kellogg Building. I had only to walk out of a side door of this building and into the front door of the McCormick Building. I roamed the halls for a bit until I saw someone to ask where the laundry room was located. I had walked right past it; not far from the door I entered. Getting the washer to accept my quarters was initially a problem; however, persistence paid off and it finally swallowed them and started pumping water. I read while I waited for the machine to finish its cycle. As soon as the clothes were spun out I moved them to a dryer. As this was going to take a little longer, I decided to make some collect phone calls. I called Richard, Katie and Dodi. I let everyone know I was A-okay. Woody would call Dodi as soon as I arrived in Lilongwe safely. Dodi would have the job of calling everyone else. If they had to get any emergency messages to me during the time I am overseas, the quickest way would be to call Woody and he would see that I receive it.

Anything else could go snail mail.

The postcards were waiting for me when I returned to my room. That was the next order of business. I finished addressing them, then started over writing messages to everyone. I ended up with twenty-eight. I had planned to send one each to Annie and Kaye but ran out of cards; actually messed up two. At this point didn't much feel I wanted to go get more. Besides the gift shop wouldn't be open. When they were stamped I took them to be mailed.

The next step was getting everything organized for traveling. I planned to check in the two large bags and carry the backpack as before. We were instructed to pack an extra change of clothing in our carry-ons for two reasons. There was the possibility of missed connections and having a longer trip than expected. Also we would need dressy clothes to wear when we arrived in Lilongwe. I decided that, besides changes of socks and underwear, I would pack one of the Sag Harbor print skirts and the silk, navy shell. They were lightweight material and wouldn't take up much space. I dug through both of the large bags and couldn't find a slip. I know I packed two; one regular length and one longer one. I suppose it won't be a problem. I checked the skirts out when I bought them and could probably get along without one. I just feel more comfortable wearing one with skirts and dresses. It bugs me that I can't find one. There is so much junk in both bags. I have no idea what I may or may not need.

After completing my little duties, I flopped on the bed and read until twelve thirty.

Day IV

Saturday, April 20, 1996

I absolutely died when I turned out the light last night. However, at six o'clock I was up and at 'em. Showered, shampooed, teeth brushed and dressed before seven. Am I excited? Is a child on Christmas morning? Everything looked as though it was as ready to go as possible at this point. I walked to the Kellogg Building to eat breakfast.

We were to leave for the airport at one o'clock. Meanwhile, they gave us luggage tags and pieces of yarn to also tie on each piece of luggage. I had already put address labels on my bags so had to remove them and start over. We had to put the street address of the Peace Corps Office in Lilongwe, not the post office box. Also I had to find Kim or Muriel to give four dollars. This to use for tipping the drivers. After seeing the luggage piled in the lobby, it was obvious, even with everyone toting their own bags to and from, that the drivers would deserve every penny of tip they received!

The last couple of hours before it was time to leave, we were all quietly talking and waiting. Several of the trainees' parents, who live in the area, were there to see their loved ones off. We were a fairly subdued group. I talked to a couple of the mothers. They seemed too young to have children old enough to be through college and volunteering two years, far from home. There weren't many tears, but I can imagine how they (the parents) feel. I used to get bluesy when Richard was in college and would go camping out west for two weeks. And Norma used to tease me about my one hundred thirty mile long umbilical cord, still attached to Mary when she married and moved to Akron. My children all cut their own umbilical cords when they were ready and I dealt with it at the time. It wasn't fun, but part of life.

The time arrived for transport to the airport; Dulles. The loading up of all the luggage was a major undertaking. We had to carry the bags from the lobby to the bus where they were stowed in the luggage compartment. The bags were all properly labeled and each had a piece of white yarn hanging from it.

After the bags were stowed all of us and our chaperones boarded the bus and we departed for the airport. I think Kim and Muriel are in charge of the passports, as we are together as a group. The luggage, not the carry-on, was placed in a large sealed container where it would remain until we were reunited with it in Lilongwe. An airline official had us lined up in a roped-off area with our carry-on luggage. Again we waited. Some of us patiently, some of us not so patiently.

Usually when I travel I make my own arrangements and tend to things myself. This business of having others guiding and being a follower is an experience I haven't dealt with for a long time. I'm thinking I'd better get used to it.

Our flight is to leave at six thirty or six forty-five. It seems hardly any time has passed since we arrived at the airport and they have us boarding. The wait was not all that long. This is a red-eye and we will be flying east all night to get into Heathrow in the morning. We are gaining or losing six hours. I'm not sure which and at this point I don't care. I'll set my watch when I arrive in London.

They haven't seated the trainees together. My seat is on the right side going in; the middle seat. On the window side is a young man with a Germanic-type accent and on the aisle side of me is a young woman.

When we are airborne the young woman tells me she is twenty-three, a nurse and works in a Baltimore trauma center. She is taking five vacation days to visit her mother. Her mother is employed by a company that sent her to England for several months. The young lady is taking the opportunity to visit her mother and see the country at the same time.

The young man doesn't have much to say, but when he speaks the accent is German, Dutch, Flemish or whatever. He seems engrossed in a physics book. He's a physicist? A student? If I were nice, I could play matchmaker and ask him if he wanted to trade

31

seats. But I'm not. Besides, what if we crashed somewhere? While the rescue workers were trying to identify the remains, they might label me "Wolfgang Schmidt", or whatever his name is. I think my children would be surprised.

The conversation lags and I start working on *Barchester Towers*. I suppose I could have started the young lady off on her job but I've seen enough of that stuff to be glad to be away from it. The conniving priests are starting to annoy me now. This book had better have a good ending or I'll throw it in the nearest trash bin. I think I need an attitude adjustment. The whole night was spent talking, reading, eating and walking to the restroom. Where else can you walk to on a flying airplane?

Day V

Sunday, April 21, 1996

I'm not sure when Sunday arrived. Sometime during the long, long night. London Heathrow is a large airport. Using the adjective "large" to describe Heathrow Airport is similar to calling the Grand Canyon a hole in the ground.

When we deplaned, we walked and walked and walked and continued to walk; were we at our destination? No. We had to stand in line. Oh, Wow! This is where we catch a shuttle to stand in line again. I'm not too sure it is a good idea to get on the thing. These crazy people are driving on the wrong side of the street. I'm waiting for a crash the whole trip to our destination; Terminal I, I think.

After we stepped off the shuttle, it was to get into another line to wait. Move a little and wait, etc. Wow! I can see where this line is going. Ah ha! Through the metal detector for us and our bags. It took awhile but we finally made it into the inner sanctum! We met the criterion which was required for entry! We were accepted! Yes! Now to find the SAA desk.

That didn't take long. Sad to say there was no one there. Inquiring of an information person, we discovered there would be no one there until three o'clock this afternoon.

Well, we have many choices of things to do. Several of the group have decided to go sightseeing in London. I'm not brave. I chose to stay right here in the terminal. No more lines than absolutely necessary. It might be fun if I didn't have a deadline to be back; not this time, however. Muriel gives everyone his or her passport and the courageous ones leave. There is an R&R area where for twenty-five dollars one can eat a continental breakfast, take a shower, shave, etc., and have a lounge chair to sleep in for the day...

Or, for seven dollars, one can take a shower. Soap, shampoo, towels are supplied. I opted for that one. I brushed my teeth in the ladies room shortly after my arrival, before I started exploring. I made a pit stop so brushed my teeth while I was there. I can see keeping my teeth clean may become a problem! So, I had a shower, changed my unmentionables and felt much better. I still wasn't tired so started to check out the terminal.

There were many interesting things to see. As in any self-respecting mall, there was a variety of shops. These had the attraction of being duty free. I bought some postcards, stamps and sent out more cards. I went to the money-changer and exchanged some dollars for British pounds, etc. After a while I became pretty good at figuring out what was what and how to add the stuff up to get the amount needed. The attendants must be used to dealing with tourists. Everyone I met was incredibly polite.

It didn't take long for everyone of our group to disappear. While I was taking a shower, as a matter of fact. Muriel was the only one around when I emerged from the rest area. She was exhausted and tried to sleep on a bench for a while; not very successfully. I think she decided to purchase the twenty-five dollar deal as she too disappeared after a while. I was enjoying myself visiting the shops, looking at merchandise on display and reminding myself that anything purchased would be carried by *moi*, and the backpack was full now. Odd thing. Lifting twenty pounds is no big deal. Even carrying that much weight isn't bad for a time. But to lug it around for hours at a time? I didn't care much for that. I guess, however, I'd best get used to it. I'll probably be wearing it on my back as if it is another article of clothing...

When I got hungry there was "McD's!" That was something I was used to. I have discovered, when I am in someplace new to me, I start looking for familiar things. Stuff I can identify with. People are people wherever one goes; but objects, even brand name merchandise, as long as they are familiar, are comforting to me. So, to Micky D's I went. The food is standardized; quality and quantity control, and all that. One could assume that McDonald's food here would be the same as McDonald's food there. I ordered a Quarter Pounder Combo, with a diet Coke. The meat is not the same. It had a taste I was not familiar with. I didn't much care for it but the mustard, pickles, catsup and onions rather hid the flavor. It wasn't the strong taste of uncastrated bull meat, but different. The Coke and fries tasted much as Coke and fries usually taste. I've run into some strange tasting Cokes in fast food places but this one was fairly "normal" tasting. I "fast food" the grandchildren a lot and getting a Coke that tastes of "Dr. Pepper", root beer or "Sprite" is not unusual. The worst one was the "Swamp-water" Cokes that Sean, Kim and I got from the Catawba Island McD's a couple of years ago. I always thought they used special water to mix those things; perhaps not.

Whenever I got tired of walking, I sat down and read. I finished *Barchester Towers*. The end was okay. All ended well and almost everyone received what he or she wanted or at least their just reward. Justice was served in other words. I started reading the next story in the book, *Miss McKenzie*. This is not an interesting story either but then I haven't really gotten into it. So far, Miss McKenzie doesn't seem likeable. Since she is the heroine apparent here, perhaps she'll do some noble deed, thus becoming my vision of a heroine. This story is not catching my fancy as I find myself watching other people as they are probably covertly watching me. I'm not doing anything interesting such as cartwheels, making faces or walking around with a cup asking for handouts; I probably blend into the woodwork and don't bear much watching.

Around two thirty, others of the group begin reappearing. We head up to the South African Airlines desk. At three o'clock someone is there. Yea! But, guess what? Our departure has been moved up two and a half hours! This may or may not be good news. The five or six trainees who went sightseeing have not returned.

Those of us who are here get ready to wait for boarding. There is a small problem. As time gets closer to boarding and some of the group may not be here to board, they must open the sealed container with all our bags and remove those belonging to the missing persons. For some reason they cannot take luggage without a corresponding passenger. We could see the fellows in charge of the baggage loading, open the box, can or whatever they call it, and start removing the luggage. We were able to watch all this from a window, hoping nothing is lost, when the missing persons arrive; just in time to board. All is well. So far.

My seat is back; way back. 56K. There is no one in the other seat. I can't believe all the room! The adrenaline is still pumping and I have been awake quite a while. Since five or six o'clock EST, yesterday morning; Saturday. Perhaps I'll sleep after take off. This is another "red-eye". We won't get into Johannesburg until tomorrow morning.

This is also a long flight. I ate, read and walked around some. I think I dozed off for about twenty minutes but mostly I'm still awake. Tired but awake.

Day VI

Monday, April 22, 1996

The flight arrived on schedule at Johannesburg. Here we are, in another airport. More duty free shops, more waiting, wandering around, etc. I had to change my clothes so I would be socially presentable for the arrival in Lilongwe. I went into the ladies restroom and into a stall. This one was larger than the one in Detroit. As a matter of fact, it was larger than any airport restroom stall I have been in at this point in my life. I did appreciate the extra room. My, by now, not so pristine, backpack went on the floor. I removed my jacket, shirt and jeans and hung them on a hook. Then retrieved the skirt and blouse from the backpack and put them on. Next, I literally stuffed the shirt, jeans and jacket into the backpack. They take up more room than the skirt and blouse! Then I looked at myself. Oh no! I can't wear the white socks and sneakers with this skirt! What was I thinking about when I packed?

So the next thing was to check out the shops. Sure enough! A duty free shop with shoes and sandals. Unfortunately, I had to buy men's sandals as they had nothing in ladies that fit me. One thing can be said about me; I have solid understanding! I convinced myself they looked "unisex". They certainly looked better than white socks and sneakers. A couple of the fellows from the group were also in the shop and the clerk assumed we were together (we were) and they were my sons (they weren't). I laughed and told him grandsons would be a better guess! To make a long story short, I put on my new sandals and stuffed the socks and sneakers into the backpack. Now it was really full! I did get it zipped. The sandals felt good (more important in my life at this point than looks) and looked okay. Now I was ready to meet the world!

They accepted my British money there but I had no idea what

it was worth exchange-wise. The sandals cost forty rand. The clerk said that was about eleven American dollars but they wouldn't accept American dollars; I paid for the sandals with my VISA card. Then I had to trust the vendors. I bought a Coke that I paid for with my British money and received change in South African rand. I am accumulating an assortment of change, half of which I have no idea what it is or what it is worth! That Coke came without ice. I had to go to the bar to get ice for it.

Our flight to Lilongwe was on time and lasted one and a half hours. My seat was the last one, on the aisle. It was one extremely clean airplane. Perhaps it was just new but I was impressed with the cleanliness. After we landed I stood up and bent over to get my backpack from under the seat. Some crew members had opened a door at the rear and the bright sun was streaming in. Oh, no! In the bright sun I may as well not be wearing a skirt! You can see right through it! What to do? What will the people think of me? Here I thought the longish skirt would be modest and keep me properly covered.

To make matters worse, after we deplaned, we had to walk quite a distance to the terminal! I kept trying to walk behind everyone, hoping no one would notice. And everyone was there! They had a huge WELCOME banner on the building and all these people were waving, watching and waiting for us. I felt so self-conscious I was only half paying attention to what was happening. To make matters worse, the terminal was small and brightly lighted by sunshine through the windows. Perhaps I am exaggerating again. I decided to pretend nothing was wrong. There were so many people there and my (sexy?) silhouette was the last thing to notice.

The whole Peace Corps staff was there, it seems, shaking hands and introducing themselves. I'll never remember everyone! Everyone seemed genuinely happy to see us and were going out of their way to sake us feel welcomed.

It was the big luggage shift scene again. This time from the center of the terminal floor to the top of a small bus. There was so much luggage, they needed a pick-up truck to carry some of it. We all crowded onto the bus. I still had my backpack and shoved it under the seat. Some of the Peace Corps staff were shepherding us. They came on the bus with us and we were off! I was near enough to the front of the bus to notice that the steering wheel and the driver were on the right side of the vehicle. We were riding on the left side of the road. I couldn't watch! I kept having an impending sense of disaster! Something similar to looking out of the passenger side window on a two-lane road high on a mountain. Habits ingrained are not easily erased. After driving forty plus years on the right side of the road, this definitely will require some adjustment. I was still excited, running on adrenaline and don't remember too much about the ride to the Kalikuti Hotel where we will be staying.

As the bus neared the hotel, the driver had to slow down as the bus was greeted by at least fifty, probably more, schoolchildren in white shirts and blouses and dark skirts and trousers. They waved, shouted and danced around the bus all the way into the Kalikuti parking lot, where we got out.

Getting off the bus was a complicated procedure because of the enthusiasm of the welcoming group who continued their dancing. Such energy! And mine was beginning to wane! Before I got off the bus, I pulled my jacket out of the backpack and tied the sleeves around my waist. That would sort of take care of my "problem". The youngsters formed a large circle to sing and dance. Then they began to draw the trainees into the circle and were encouraging them to clap and dance. They tried to get me to join them but I resisted getting into the circle. Rather I stood at the side lines, holding several bags for others while they danced. I sure didn't want to start wiggling my hips! As it was, I needed to continue pulling at my jacket sleeves so it stayed in place. After these festivities, we were given our room assignments.

My room-mate was Christine, a pretty, kind, thoughtful, young lady with long dark brown hair. We had to share the door key as there was only one. The room had two single beds, a table and a chair. The bathroom was large and the closets were small. We put our bags in the room. I dug my jeans out of the backpack and pulled them on under my skirt. Tomorrow or later, I would search both bags until I found the slips!

We were given instructions and our agenda for the week. Also had the opportunity to talk to some of the people who would be taking us through our training. All of the Malawians speak excellent English. I just hope I can do this thing! Even "Muli bwanji?" doesn't want to roll off my tongue! Perhaps I am being self-conscious?

Dinner was buffet style in the dining room. After we had our food on our plates, we made our way to a table. The tables in one part of the dining room were large, round and seated six or seven persons. Most of us made our way to one of these. There were waiters who came to the table to ask what we wanted to drink. I chose tea into which I dropped a Nutra Sweet tablet. The food was quite tasty although I'm not sure what some of it was.

In the evening, we were given our rabies and typhoid shots. This is always "fun". We each took our turn and each person's immunization record had to be updated. The vaccines are stored and carried in a beverage cooler. This was all taken care of by our nurse, Lucy. I did learn one name. I think she will be in charge of our health care. She and a medical officer whose name escapes me. She wasn't there.

I talked for a while with some of the staff and started to fall asleep. I decided to excuse myself and leave before I embarrassed myself by falling asleep talking. I have been known to do that and not remembered a thing I said! The adrenaline must have dried up or the receptors were failing to react. I had been awake, except for about twenty minutes during the flight from London to Johannesburg, since early Saturday morning. Wow!

I found my way back to my room, let myself in and got ready for bed. Christine came back before I fell asleep, then left again. I warned her that I snore, and suggested she tell me to roll over if I kept her awake. After I settled myself in bed, I went immediately to sleep.

Christine lost part of her luggage somewhere in transit. It was not at the Lilongwe Airport with the rest of the stuff. We decided it was left at Heathrow when they opened the canister to remove the luggage of the missing group members. She was one of them. They are checking to see if it can be found.

At some point Christine came in and went to bed. Apparently, I was sawing wood with much enthusiasm as she shook my foot and said, "You're snoring." I apologized, rolled over and went back to sleep.

At about one o'clock I awakened with a mosquito buzzing by my ear. I tried swatting at it with no luck. I didn't want to turn on the light as it would probably awaken Christine and I suspected she hadn't been in bed long. I pulled the sheet over my head and hoped the mosquito would go away. They haven't given us mosquito netting for our beds yet...

Day VII

Tuesday, April 23, 1996

Guess what? I woke up at daybreak to the sound of honking geese! There must be a home outside the hotel where they raise geese. I didn't see much around the building yesterday when we arrived. We naturally entered the front of the building and the parking area is partially enclosed by a wall and beautiful vegetation; flowering shrubs or whatever. My room is at the side and back from the front entrance. I had attempted to look out of our window but couldn't see much. I'll need to explore a little and figure out how to get around this building. Plus, after the initial greeting dance, etc., I had been inside this building.

There are multiple mosquito bites on my forearms and hands. They are smaller than most mosquito bites I have seen before and they don't itch much. My friend, the ear buzzer, must have notified her friends it was party time! Party they did! Drinking themselves silly! At my expense! And I was sleeping! The windows have screens which means the mosquitoes must be small enough to get through the holes. I just hope they are not anopheles. My next Mefloquine is due on Thursday and the stuff I have has expired!

When I went into the bathroom to get cleaned up, I noticed the windows were open and had no screens. No wonder the mosquitoes thought we had rolled out the red carpet! Tonight we will either shut the windows or the bathroom door.

After taking a sponge bath, brushing my teeth, etc., I walked to the dining room for breakfast. Mine consisted of tea and toast. I carry my little Nutra Sweet dispenser in my pocket to sweeten the tea. I was joined by several other trainees. The conversation centered around mosquitoes, the rooms, sleeplessness for some, etc. I shared that I had been awakened by the poultry outside my window. The fellows laughed so hard at this, I was puzzled.

"What's so funny?" I questioned them. One of the group choked out, "Poultry!" nudged the fellow sitting next to him and they were off again into their inexplicable hilarity. When they were finally able to compose themselves, they explained that my "geese" were huge black and white crows! It was funny! These birds are not as large as geese but larger than normal-sized chickens. They have black heads and backs and snow white feathers on their breasts. I had seen a couple yesterday walking around the courtyard. Hey! I'm in a strange country and don't know they don't raise poultry and livestock in the city. Nothing will surprise me.

Today the classes start. The language is what I'm concerned about, If I don't learn it, I don't get an assignment…

We are divided into groups of five or six for language. We will be taught the language spoken by the natives in the place where we are assigned. I am to be assigned to Kasungu and am learning Chichewa. The trainees assigned in the north are being taught Chitumbuka.

Stella is the instructor for our group. She teaches English in a girls' training school. They are on break now so she is with us. She is a tiny person. She reminds me of Vicie, a nurse assistant I worked with many years ago, who died in childbirth. I didn't tell Stella this, but a couple of times I caught myself before I called her "Vicie". The resemblance is uncanny. The same bone structure; she even walks the same way.

Stella is very kind and encouraging. We practiced the first lesson in our book. Our textbook has four authors: Sabina Itimu, Crosby Mtawali, Shadreck Chakwawa and Chris Mkwapatira. Chris and Sabina made the language tape. We were introduced to the other two, Crosby and Shadreck, but I'm not sure who is who yet.

We are to be going to the market one day this week. Stella is trying to teach us how to shop and ask directions in Chichewa…

"Msika uli kuti?"

"Msika uli apo."

"Lankhulani, pangongo pangongo. Iyayi! Eya! Help!"

I still have trouble with "Muli bwanji?" Now I must learn, "Mwadzuka bwanji?" and "Mwaswera bwanji?" Ndi kudwala! I'm not really sick, but I feel overwhelmed. I wonder if I memorized these phrases, would it help? Unfortunately, I don't understand what someone is saying to me. I could say one of my memorized phrases to someone, but wouldn't understand their reply. The trainers are all so cute! One of the fellows called me "agogo" (grandmother).

The chitenji is a plain piece of fabric, about two yards or two meters long. It is a most versatile thing. Women tie the ends together after extending it under one arm and over the opposite shoulder. This forms a sling so they can carry babies and young children and keep their hands free. It can also be wrapped around the waist and fastened by rolling the ends under. One must keep one's feet spread apart while wrapping it, as one would hobble and walking would be most difficult. Wearing it this way or fastened the same way but over the chest acts as an apron and is always worn over regular clothing.

A third way to use the chitenji is to tie blankets, baskets, or multiple items inside. This is accomplished by placing whatever is being wrapped in the center and tying the opposing corners together. Now one has a neat bundle that can be carried on the head. This enables one to walk long distances with the hands free for something else.

Another use for it is to gather it together width-wise in one hand and make loops around the hand until you have a thick flat pad. This can be placed on the head to act as a cushion while carrying an extra heavy load such as a large container of water. The chitenji can also be worn around the head as a turban.

Men occasionally use the chitenji as a wrap-around. The fellows cross it in the front and tie two corners behind the neck. Men would not wear this out in public but perhaps at home after bathing.

Stella informed us we will want to purchase a chitenji when we go to the market, as we will need this in the village. "Bwanji, bwanji chitenji?" we will ask. "Fifty kwatcha basi" should be the answer. We should not pay more than that for a chitenji. At fifteen kwatcha to a dollar, that means the chitenji costs a little more than three dollars in our money. However, we must deal in kwatcha. All of our money was collected and locked up, along with the credit cards, etc., at the Peace Corps headquarters for safe keeping until we leave Malawi. The classes go on. I haven't recuperated from the flight yet and there is so much to learn before we go to the village.

There was a reception this evening from six until seven thirty. We met more people. Everyone is so helpful but my circuits are overloaded. I did have the opportunity to talk to some of the trainers who will be going to the village with us.

They had hors d'oeuvres as well as an assortment of beverages. I had two pieces of meat on a toothpick and a half a bottle of warm Coke. The second piece of meat was a square of approximately one inch and a quarter inch thick. It was broiled chicken liver. Chicken liver is the one thing in the world that, if I swallow it, will try to come up on me. Actually there are two, the other being oysters. I took a small bite of it, fortunately. As soon as I discover what it is, it is panic city. I will swallow it and pray it doesn't come back. It tried, but by force of will, it stayed put. I walked around with the liver on a toothpick and my Coke. By taking a swallow of the Coke, apparently the stomach was convinced the offending substance had left. After that I wasn't interested in eating anything else.

We were to have dinner in the dining room after the reception. I didn't much feel like eating anything and was tired. I had hoped we would have a day to recuperate from the jet lag but it is not to be. The schedule for the rest of the week looks pretty full so I imagine the pace will continue. Sitting down listening to lectures is as tiring as sitting in an airplane. Even the tea breaks don't help much. I went to my room, ate three shortbreads I had purchased at Heathrow. That should hold me until morning.

Before I went to bed I closed the bathroom door. Christine and I discussed this earlier and decided on that course of action. There is a ceiling fan in the room and with it on it doesn't get so hot and stuffy. Christine was out bonding somewhere so I crashed after practicing talking to myself in Chichewa. I can't even practice speaking with Christine as she is learning Chitumbuka. She is going to the Northern District, I to the Central District.

Day VIII

Wednesday, April 24, 1996

Here I am, starting my second week. Some of the volunteers are here to help with our orientation. I am happy to see some gray hair! Three ladies, Mary, Jane and Bobbie. I feel better already. Not that I was feeling bad but the orientation is geared mostly for young people. I haven't lost my serenity, but much of what is said is just good sense.

This morning Jane gave a talk on stress and substance abuse. I thought it was quite effective but who knows what reaction the others had. The stress, I have a handle on. However, if this pace continues and I don't get rest, who knows? Most of it was review for me. I do take time to meditate every morning and sometimes at night again. Also, if I wake up during the night it keeps my mind quiet. I have been more wakeful than I normally am, but with everything happening it is probably just my good old adrenaline. Pat, a nurse, told me that if I got stressed out and needed a shoulder she was available. That was thoughtful of her. At this point I am okay. One day at a time. It isn't the destination, it's the journey and I'll not pass this way again.

This afternoon our language group walked to the market. This is the first time I have been out of the hotel since we arrived. It was a learning experience and an opportunity to see a little of Lilongwe. With Stella as our guide and kwatcha in our pockets, we set out.

After we walked away from the hotel we walked on footpaths. Most of the buildings were brick. Some of the places had high brick walls around them that had broken shards of glass embedded in concrete on the top. Climbing over the wall would be a poor decision. It appeared rather intimidating. I imagine it would be an inexpensive, durable and effective method of protecting one's property.

Initially, we didn't see many people as we walked. As we neared the highway, the number of walkers increased. Of course we were cause for stares with our white skin.

It was about a mile to the market after we came to the paved road. No sidewalks; just footpaths on either side of the road. The footpaths are heavily traveled. We met many walkers and many passed us. Occasionally, we were passed by a bicycle rider. We also passed the occasional vendor selling produce in small amounts along the path. One young woman had a small pile of peanuts for sale...

The market was at a busy intersection. The one street seemed to end at the one we were walking along. Watching for vehicular traffic was tricky for me. The cars were not where I expected them to be. I get carried away mulling over in my mind, they are driving on the wrong side of the road and it isn't right! We made it across that street and into the market.

It reminded me of a flea market in the U.S., but dirty and unsanitary. There were drainage ditches that were filled with all types of debris. And the flies were plentiful. There were vendors selling everything from ready to eat food, clothing, pots, pans, dishes, other household needs, shoes, meat, fish and an endless array too numerous to itemize. The space between the vendors was narrow and as we went further into the market. I was afraid I would lose Stella. To make things more confusing, people were going in both directions through the aisles that barely accommodated one person!

After we looked around for a while, Stella led us to where we could buy a chitenji. The vendors at this place spoke English but Stella directed us on what and how to purchase ours. These were only forty-five kwatcha, five kwatcha less than she had advised us to pay. She had told us not to pay more than fifty kwatcha. After we had our chitenji, we started moving through the market.

We passed some ladies who were making wigs and Stella stopped to exchange some conversation with them. I became interested in watching them and did not notice when Stella and the others started to walk on. I panicked when I looked up and didn't see Stella! After some uncomfortable moments, I found her as well as some trainees who were not in our language group.

George, the only fellow in our group, met some of the fellows from another group and switched loyalty. He went with the guys. He was tired of girl talk! We did a little inter-group switcheroo and continued walking through the market. We came to an area where the aisles were wider and walking about became a little easier.

Stella also suggested we get some rubber flip-flops to wear for bathing and very casual wear. A vendor who was selling them for twenty-two kwatcha let us have them for twenty, thanks to Stella. As we wandered through the aisles, I saw some large fish covered with flies. (Now I see why we are instructed to wash and cook everything we eat!) I was ready to leave at this point but had to wait for the rest. I would never find my way back to the Kalikuti without my diminutive mentor!

The walk back to the Kalikuti was not without its excitement. Crossing the street could have been hazardous to our health. At least to the health of Stella and one of the other trainees. Part of our group had made it safely to the opposite side of the street while some were somewhat behind. From seemingly nowhere, a motorbike came speeding around a curve, barely missing the walkers! We were still somewhat shaken when we arrived back at the hotel.

Dinner in the dining room was fun. The market did nothing to lessen my appetite. I was hungry and ate nsima, rice with a sauce from liver, spinach or some type of greens, carrots and a salad consisting of green peppers, tomatoes and some other things I couldn't identify. The waiters came around and took orders for beverages. Everyone else at my table ordered a soft drink and I ordered tea. The soft drinks came but no tea. The staff was so busy that there was no way I was going to get it either. Someone else probably got my tea!

What made the meal special was it was Barbara's birthday. Someone had ordered a cake. We had a party, sang "Happy Birthday' and ate cake.

This morning when the attendant did our room, he only left one towel. We couldn't let that be. Christine and I each wanted our own. On one of my trips past the reception desk, I requested another towel. When I returned after dinner, we had two towels *and* a bath mat!

I'm having trouble getting used to the early darkness. I keep thinking it is going to rain or that it is later than it actually is. In Ohio the days were getting longer. Now that I am south of the Equator, the days are getting shorter.

It was about seven forty-five when I returned to my room. I need to study, but instead wrote a couple of letters; one to Richard and one to Katie.

Day IX

Thursday, April 25, 1996

Another day of classes on everything we need to know for survival in Malawi or any other place with primitive conditions. Wow! My brain is bursting! More language, culture, disease prevention. How to treat food and water. Water must be boiled. Better yet, filter it, then boil it. Stay away from water with snails. Don't have unprotected sex. P.V.C.s have contracted HIV and other diseases of the sexually promiscuous; the list goes on...

They put on a skit about the proper use of the chimbudzi or latrine. They were funny but got the point across. One must always clap the hands or make some noise when approaching the "chim". If a person is using the chim, they are able to let you know. To maintain their privacy, you leave and return later.

The chim, for the skit, was a canvas tent affair, about four feet high, pointed at the top with a base large enough to accommodate a squatting adult. The tent had a flap closure. The trainers demonstrated both methods of approaching the chim. The proper way was quiet and "oh, hum". But when the approaching person put his head into the opening without the clapping or the noise, out jumped one of the trainers with much ado, pulling up his trousers and making much of this interference. We all laughed but the lesson was learned.

The volunteers who have come to help with our orientation have a wide variety of backgrounds. One fellow is a dietitian. He had a class on maintaining a nutritious diet with available food.

This is Mefloquine day. Lucy, the nurse, gave me a package of tablets that she said had not expired. I took one of those first thing in the morning; I had given her the expired tablets. We have sort of conquered the mosquitoes by keeping the bathroom door shut. They don't do much during the day. I still have my bites but they don't itch. The P.C. also issued us netting for our beds; however, there is nothing to hold or tie them up with so at this point are useless. Someone is supposed to give us some string. I imagine it is low priority.

The weather is so pleasant. It has rained a little twice, but not long enough to get things wet. I discovered a clothes line in a small courtyard. I hang my unmentionables on hangers in the bathroom. It is highly improper to hang them where someone may see them. Socks, skirts, shirts, blouses, etc., I hang on the outside line. They dry rather quickly. The trainers left gift packages in our rooms the day we arrived. These contained bar soap, laundry soap, and toothpaste. All these things have been most useful.

The laundry must be done by hand in the bathroom wash bowl. I could use the bathtub, I suppose, but that wastes so much water and also involves bending and stooping. The stooping I'll avoid when I can and the basin is a good height. If there is a laundry here, I have no idea where it might be. Also, wouldn't have someone do mine anyway. The soap they gave us has come in handy and works well for this. It is good soap.

There is a courtyard surrounded on three sides by the guest rooms and the fourth side is where the lobby, kitchen, dining rooms, meeting rooms, etc., are located. The walkway in front of the rooms has an overhanging roof with the obligatory posts and a low wall rather than a railing between the posts. The posts have vines growing on them, also along the roof edge of the overhang. Some of these are flowering. The courtyard is made of concrete but has some trees to provide shade. There are tables and chairs where we may sit to enjoy the fresh air and sunshine. In my spare time, of which there is little, I like to sit there and study. The courtyard where I hang my laundry is smaller than this and is connected with this one by a walkway on the opposite side from my room.

I have in the past couple of days managed to explore some of the hotel. My first thought when I entered was "Wow! This is something from a 'thirties' movie!" I don't know if the building is older than me, or if it just appears that way. It is comforting in a way; it gives me a feeling of nostalgia. There is a large meeting room where we had our first classes, meetings and the reception.

There are "French" doors opening to the verandah, which in turn faces the parking lot. It was here, on the verandah, where I stood watching the children dance the day I arrived. We have sat on the verandah during our language class and often congregate there at teatime. This is the front of the building. Another door, to the right of the verandah doors, coming from the parking lot, leads to the reception desk and a gift shop. There are maze-like halls that lead to the dining rooms, smaller meeting rooms and outside to the courtyards and guest rooms.

I had lunch with Bobbie, Mary C. and Chris, the head trainer. Bobbie and Mary are volunteers, my age, completely different personalities, both delightful. Bobbie made a statement to the effect that she didn't think her village stay during training needed to be so long. This was a couple of years ago as she is about to finish her term. She felt it was just like the depression in the U.S. She lived through the depression once and that was enough! Her saying that reinforced my first impression so perhaps my feeling was not too far off the mark.

I wonder what the village will be like. I was a small child during the thirties, born in 1932. I knew we weren't wealthy but I never felt deprived. Kaye and Toni felt differently about it; they were older, in school and more aware. Dad was philosophical but he had lived through more than the depression on a farm; perhaps three wars and a widowed mother trying to manage the farm after the death of his father. His attitude was more one of acceptance; if you don't have it, tighten your belt. I'll find out when I get there...

Day X

Friday, April 26, 1996

More classes; malaria and STDs. The Peace Corps area physician gave us those. That was a misleading sentence! He didn't give us the diseases; he taught the classes! He seems young (doesn't everyone?) but has been in the Peace Corps for a while. He is in charge of the Peace Corps volunteers' health for several African countries. Our regular health officer, Neni, whom everyone speaks of but we haven't seen, is at a conference, on vacation or some obscure place for some obscure purpose. He is filling in. Lucy, the nurse, and Mr. Chimzizi, our medical officer, will be going to the village with us.

I didn't sleep well last night. I had some colorful dreams that I can't remember much about. There were lots of green leaves grass, bright flowers, colorful dresses, etc. The colors were vivid but the dream was senseless. I suppose I should appreciate being so entertained.

This is the wind-up of our week in Lilongwe. We will be going to the village on Monday. I have been sitting in class all week and my feet have been swollen since the eternal flights here. After I finish writing, I think I'll prop my feet up high and see if that won't drain some of the fluid out. The swelling isn't bad but I don't like it and I don't like what it indicates.

I finished reading my book, did my laundry and will study for a while. Christine is out for the evening as are most of the others, trainees and trainers. The volunteers who have been helping out with our orientation have arranged an event of singing, dancing and general partying at a local night spot. If I were forty years younger it might sound fun; I've been there, done that. I've passed that phase and learning Chichewa has more appeal. Christine took the key so I won't need to worry about getting up to let her in after I go to bed.

Day XI

Saturday, April 27, 1996

This has been a fairly quiet day. We finished our preping sessions, the medical interviews, ate the usual meals, etc. There is a convention of some sort going on. The place is packed with well-dressed business types; doctors? lawyers? Getting served in the dining room is more difficult and we have been using the smaller meeting rooms for our classes.

I am going to be assigned to the District Hospital in Kasungu after I finish my training. All I know about it is it is in the Central District and Chichewa is the village language.

I packed my backpack to take to the village. Enough under-wear to last a week, three changes of clothing, my little rubber flip-flops, shampoo, *slips*, toothpaste, toothbrush, my eye drops, nail clippers, files, comb, brush, books, paper, pens, stamps, envelopes and a small bottle with some Woolite. I put the detergent the trainers gave me in a plastic bag and decided to leave it with the things I would not be taking to the village. I also have a bag that fastens around the waist that has two quart-sized bottles on either side. These for drinking water. I will fill them with drinking water before we leave for the village. I hope it lasts until I see where and how I will be getting my drinking water. The bag holds the small things I am taking; the nail file, clippers, comb, brush and the small bottles of shampoo, etc. Also two large men's handkerchiefs and a flashlight. I think I remembered everything they told us.

Day XII

Sunday, April 28, 1996

This is another fairly quiet day. I am working on my language. I was wakeful during the night. Conversations in Chichewa kept running through my mind. It wasn't going to hurt anything so I didn't try to stop them. In actual practice, I can say some things, but when someone speaks to me, I am not able to understand enough to make the appropriate response. I have memorized the conversations in the book and, if I am talking to myself, I do fairly well. Speaking to someone else doesn't come off too well. A couple of volunteers who are helping with our training put on a skit speaking Chichewa and it sounded good. I wonder if I'll ever get to that point. I guess I'd better or I won't get an assignment!

When one of the trainers speaks to me in Chichewa, I am stumped. One will say to me, "Mwaswera bwanji?" My response should be, "Ndaswerea bwino. Kaya inu?" What generally happens is, "Oh, oh! He or she didn't say 'muli'. Now how do I respond to 'mwaswera?'" By this time I am flustered because the proper response is not on the tip of my tongue. There is a time lapse that is embarrassing for me before I finally get it out. They are always patient but I should know this; it is the first lesson!

I enjoy sitting in the courtyard studying. It is usually comfortable and sunny. Although, with the conference going on, it is more crowded with people than earlier in the week. Sometimes the tables and chairs aren't available. The vines and plants growing around are lush and lovely, but unhappily for me, I am unable to identify any of them. I have that problem when I go to California or Florida, to a point. This, however, is more so. I did see poinsettia trees growing along the highway as we drove here from the airport, but those were the only growing things that looked familiar.

The day has been pretty routine; bathing, laundry, tooth care, meals, etc. Tomorrow is the day we go to the village.

Day XIII

Monday, April 29, 1996

This is the day for the big push. The day we leave for the village. We pack those things that we are taking with us. The rest of our belongings are to be stored at Vyrle Owens' home until we get our assignments. I just hope I have everything I need. We all had to move our bags, that were to be stored, to the lobby and from there to a room in the hotel where they would be retrieved later.

Once again we had been provided with mosquito netting for our beds, but we had nothing to hold up the corners. Someone said they will give us twine. I suppose that will come later. Also, we were each issued a medical kit. It contained all sorts of good things; a thermometer, aspirin, antibiotics, acetaminophen, condoms, dressings, iodine tablets and instruction books plus much more. I put my Mefloquine tablets in mine as well as some butterscotch candies I had purchased at Heathrow, not opened yet, and a pack of sugarless gum that I had been carrying since I left home.

I filled my water bottles, strapped the little carrier around my waist, shouldered my backpack, picked up my sleeping bag and boarded the bus. Well, not quite. The backpack along with everyone else's was loaded on top of the bus, then tied down. All I took on the bus with me was my little nurse kit and the water bottle carrier. I stashed the kit under the seat in front of me, sat down by a window, propped my feet on the little nurse kit and was ready to go. The seats were narrow and Muriel, my poor seat-mate, had to hang out into the aisle.

When we are all packed in like sardines in a can, we are off to God Knows where. The trainers know, the driver knows; I guess that is all that is important. I'm not sure what direction we are going but I think it is north. It had to have been in circles; we drove around Lilongwe for a while and arrived at the Peace Corps headquarters! Well!

Two of our group are returning home. This fact was unknown to many of us, including *moi*. The one fellow was not responding well to the Mefloquine and hadn't slept for over a week. The other was a young woman who decided this wasn't what she wanted. So we left them there. We were off to the village; they to the U.S. I wasn't aware there was a problem with her although some of the others were. I did know he was having problems with insomnia as it had continued for so long. Many of us were having crazy dreams but hadn't heard of any other side effects from the Mefloquine.

It was sad leaving them at headquarters. I know the ordeal I went through during the process of being accepted as a Peace Corps trainee. To get all the way to the destination and need to change course would be a difficult decision to make. This is also sad for the rest of us as we are becoming a "family".

The trip to the village proved to be a long but interesting one. The landscape appeared generally flat or "rolling" with "mountains" jutting at intervals. Occasionally, we could see clusters of thatch-roofed houses in the distance but none close enough to determine much other than they must be villages; but not ours. There was an occasional store or place of business along the highway but mostly vegetation, tall grass, flowering trees, small trees, and land undulating into the distance. It was beautiful but not the lush green I was accustomed to in N.W. Ohio and S.E. Michigan. Of course this is autumn here; perhaps it is different in the summer. There were a few clouds, but mostly sun and blue sky.

We also passed roads leading from the highway often with signs indicating a school or government-related compound. I can't remember most of them. We passed Kasungu but I couldn't see anything about it. Actually we passed the road to Kasungu.

The trip had a couple of incidents before we got to the village. One of our group, who had been sick before we left, became progressively worse as the trip went on. We made a stop for a while so that she could have some much needed care. Some of us got off the bus and walked around a bit while we were waiting. Later, we were stopped by some military types who had set up a roadblock. They didn't detain us long, however, and we were on our way.

The bus driver turned off the highway to the left and onto a bumpy dirt road. I seem to have lost my ability to judge distances but we seemed to drive along this road a long way. It probably wasn't more than a mile or a mile and a half but it seemed to me a long distance.

Finally, we arrive at what must be the village center. There is a large building with open space for windows and doors; but no glass or doors. A shelter house? No. It is the school. There are benches inside.

Now we meet the villagers. We are introduced to the people in authority; the schoolteacher and others. It seems there is more than one headman but I'm not sure. Much of this is going over my head. There are speeches by our trainers in English and in Chichewa and Chitumbuka by the village elders. These are translated by our trainers so that we can understand.

The village children put on a program of dancing. The girls dance. This is amazing; to watch those little fannies move in seemingly impossible motions to rhythms thumped on drums by several of the young men. One little cutie, who didn't appear to be more than four or five years old, kept stopping to refasten her chitenji as it came undone while she was dancing. The older girls didn't seem to have that problem.

There was also a performance by the village medicine man and some of his apprentices. This consisted of an acrobatic type dance, also to the beat of drums. I was impressed but also somewhat disappointed in that their costumes were not as bright and colorful as those I had seen in pictures. The face masks were frightening. One in particular. When he turned to face me and made eye contact, I thought, "Holy Toledo! That could inspire terror in the heart of anyone!" Which it was meant to do. The medicine man has much authority in the village. People threw kwatcha and tambala at them while they were dancing.

After the performance we were introduced to our families. I would be staying with Bambo and Mayi Nyasulu. Mayi Nyasulu told me her name was Ruby. She was holding a chubby cherub named Stella who was about twelve to eighteen months old. This was her granddaughter, her son's little girl.

One little episode that made me hesitant to interact with the little one occurred in the receiving line formed by the villagers as we left the bus. I would guess there were anywhere from one hundred to two hundred people lined up to shake hands and say, "Muli bwanji?" There were many young women holding small children in the receiving line. The little ones were particularly interested in seeing us. Many of the children had never seen a white person before and here was one with gray hair! They watched us, wide-eyed and precious. I made the mistake of making eye contact and smiling at one. He was terrified, howled and hid his little face against his mother's shoulder. I won't make that mistake again. The older children seem to take the whole thing in their stride. I guess that statement that the children may not have seen a white face is inaccurate as I noticed a village boy of about ten or eleven who is albino; blond hair and all.

After introductions, my "mother", who is younger than me, led me to what is to be my home for the next several weeks. Blessedly she had a young woman, Beatie, same name as me, carry my backpack. I felt bad about that as she was quite tiny, but "Mother" insisted. Beatie balanced the unwieldy backpack on her head and was extremely graceful as she walked along. Someone else carried my sleeping bag and I carried my medical kit. I'm being treated as royalty, wow!

We walked along the dirt road the bus brought us in on. I was helped at times by a delightful child of about four or five, another granddaughter, named Thandi. She would try to carry my medical kit for a bit but after feeling the weight she was satisfied to hold the handle along with me until something more interesting caught her fancy. She would return to the task at hand briefly, then off again being busy as only a little girl can be busy.

The walk seemed to last forever. I normally walk rapidly but it seems I am going to make some changes here. Many of the villagers were going in the same direction. Some with their new adoptive "children", the other trainees. It was great being outside and moving. Conversation was limited as my "mother" did not speak much English and my Chichewa was practically useless. "Muli bwanji?" and "Zikomo," which meant "How are you?" and

"Thank you," respectively, were all I knew What have I gotten myself into? But everyone is so kind. I do pick up a word or two once in a while. Thandi called Mayi "agogo" – grandmother. That was neat.

After we walked probably a mile, although it seemed farther, we arrived at the main highway, crossed it and turned right. Continued on farther. There were some mud or clay houses along the way, about four or five. These had thatched roofs. Then we arrived at a brick house with a large flowering bush in the front. The house had louvered glass windows, a porch that was concealed by trees and a corrugated metal roof. This was to be my home! How lucky can I get? Wow!

After we arrived at the house, I was shown to my room. The floor of the house was concrete. There were rugs on the floor in the living room which we entered through the front door. The living room had two windows with louvered glass. The furniture was simple, probably made by a village carpenter, but comfortable. There was a couch and comfortable chairs, a kerosene lamp, pictures on the walls and books on bookshelves. The living room was arranged so that the chairs formed a divider from the dining area. Here there was a large table and chairs. At the dining end of the room were two doors at right angles to each other. The one opened into the master bedroom where Mayi and Bambo slept and the other door led to a hall that led to the back door. There was a bedroom on either side of the hall. My room was on the right going into the hall from the dining room. There was a curtain hung on twine over the doorway. The room was small; a single-sized bed and small table on which sat an arrangement of the red flowers from the front tree. There were two windows; one on each outside wall, with shutters. One shutter was closed but the other opened into the backyard. My bed was a simple wood frame made of 2x2's, elevated from the floor about eighteen inches and supported at the corners by 2x4's. This was covered by a sheet of heavy plastic or something similar to naugahyde. I put my backpack on the table and my sleeping bag on the bed. Bambo told me to close the shutter when I went to bed.

It was only about four thirty or five o'clock by this time. Jane Bonine, one of the administrators in Malawi, was also staying with the Nyasulus. Jane works for the State Department and is second in charge under Vyrle Owens, the director. I was so thankful for Jane's presence. She acted as my liaison and interpreter. Bambo speaks English well but Mayi does not speak much. We sat in the living room and visited for a while. Then they served tea with eggs and fried potatoes. The potatoes were cut in strips. French fry style but larger. It was delicious and I ate everything on my plate, which was a lot!

Then I discovered that was tea. Dinner came later! By the time dinner was served there was no way I could force myself to eat. But I am getting ahead of myself.

There is no electricity in the village. There is also no indoor plumbing. I was given the grand tour. Out the back door and down a step and I was in the backyard. The yard is enclosed by a high grass fence. The tall grass is tied in bunches and attached to a frame of poles. The yard itself was bare packed with brown-red dirt. There was a small area where some grass grew and Mayi had flowers planted by the fence.

A brick building stood about fifteen or twenty feet to the left going out of the door. This had a thatched roof and was actually several buildings together. The first was the kitchen where there were fireplaces to cook. Next to that was a storage room where they kept some foodstuffs such as ofa; next to that was the bathhouse.

At the end of the long brick building was a smaller building of sticks, raised up where the chickens could roost at night. The chickens had the run of the yard of course. They were all beautiful black chickens.

As you go out the back door and walk left, not going to the cook house, but beyond, there is an opening in the fence that leads beside the house, to the front yard, the neighbor, who happens to be one of the Nyasulus' sons, and on to the highway. But to continue in the backyard, just inside the opening, sits another small building. This one is probably five feet or perhaps six feet square and about four feet high. This is the goat shed where they are kept at night.

We continue walking and the fence sort of gives way to the neighbors' backyard on the left and on the right is a large shelter where Bambo hangs tobacco to dry. We continue walking and finally come to the outer limits and the chimbudzi. This is about the distance of half a football field from the back door.

The chimbudzi (latrine) is a brick building with a thatched roof and a concrete floor. The concrete is several inches thick and the building is situated over a deep hole. Fortunately, we can't see how deep. In the center of the floor is a hole about six or eight inches in diameter. That's it. There is a shoe box with some old newspapers nearby. The plumbing. The building is clean; no odor. This is my home for the next six weeks.

It has been an exciting day and by this time I am bushed. I could stand in a corner and fall asleep. We haven't had dinner yet! I begged to be excused from dinner; it hasn't been two hours since tea when I overate. I asked if I may just go to bed. I felt I was being ungracious but I was feeling tired as I was that first evening in Lilongwe. I thought that if I fell asleep while everyone was gaily making conversation, I would disgrace myself completely!

I took my flashlight and made my way to the chimbudzi. That wasn't as bad as I thought it would be. I undressed by flashlight beam, got into my nightshirt, then crawled into my sleeping bag and was almost asleep when who should arrive but Chris and Crosby, the trainers general. They had foam mattresses, sheets, blankets, pillows, candles and matches. Oh, and more toilet paper. So, I got up, wrapped my chitenji around me and started over again. I still didn't have twine for the mosquito netting so figured, "What the heck." Bambo said there weren't many mosquitoes this time of year so I didn't worry too much. I was too tired to think about it much; besides, I was taking my Mefloquine. I put my mattress on the bed, made the bed, turned out the flashlight and tried again.

I slept well, although I did wake up a couple of times, I went right back to sleep. Bambo has a clock in the living room that plays a few measures of old-timey melodies such as "Long, Long Ago" and "Santa Lucia" on the hour; then strikes the hour. So, I knew what time it was without turning on my flashlight. It's possible the clock was waking me up but it was a comforting sound.

Day XIV

Tuesday, April 30, 1996

I woke up before daylight with the rooster alarm clock. Malawian roosters do not crow, "Cocka-doodle-doo!" as ours do, but, "Ko-ko-li-li-ko!" It is interesting but the Chichewa translation is more accurate. We learned a song in class that starts "Tambala walira, ko-ko-li-li-ko". "Tambala" is rooster; "walira" translates as "cries". In English we would say, "The rooster cries cocka-doodle-doo". It has been many years since I have been awakened by a rooster crowing. It is a pleasant sound; for me anyway. Not everyone feels that way, I'm sure. I could hear people stirring around outside but not everyone seemed to be up.

Jane is my guide and she patiently explains things for me. I wonder how the others are making out without a personal translator and guide. I am so fortunate! Beatie introduced me to the bathhouse. I took my clean underwear, soap, shampoo, conditioner, comb, toothbrush, toothpaste, wash cloth, and towel, put on my flip-flops, wrapped my chitenji around me and tied the corners behind my neck and was ready! I tie the chitenji behind my neck as I haven't mastered the art of doing it properly as the Malawian ladies do; it comes undone, just as the little dancer's did yesterday. I suspect she'll be keeping hers fastened before I do! I am working on it...

In the bathhouse is a large plastic tub half full of pleasantly warm water. There is a flat stone where I can place my bag with the soap, etc., and a clothes line where I can hang my towel and clothing. There is a small drain hole at the back.

The first thing I do is brush my teeth. This presents a small problem as I neglected to bring water to rinse either my mouth or the brush. I haven't brushed my teeth since I left Lilongwe yesterday morning and it feels as though the moss has set up permanent residence. I do what I can. Brush and spit. I spit by the little drain hole but of course the spit doesn't go anywhere; just sits there. Yuk! I'll be lucky to have any teeth in my head by the time I return to the States!

I strip off the nightshirt. This is one of those oversized T-shirts with raglan sleeves, calf length, easy on, easy off. First I bend over and put the top of my head in the water to wet my hair, put some shampoo on my hand and rub that into a lather. Back into the water to rinse out the soap. So far, so good. I put a little conditioner into my palm and rub that through my wet hair. The hair is done. The rest of the bath is a sponge number and I feel much cleaner when I am finished. I put on my clean underwear and run the comb through my hair. Very carefully I empty the water from the tub. I start pouring too fast; the little drain hole can't accommodate the rush so I slow it down. The disgusting blob of spit obligingly goes out the drain with the water.

I didn't bring deodorant with me. I figured if I smelled bad, so would everyone else. I was as clean as I could be. I tidied up the bathhouse, pulled on the nightshirt, tied the chitenji back on, picked up my belongings and headed back to my room. The flip-flops I only removed long enough to wash my feet and they, because they were wet, managed to accumulate sand from the yard. I had to wipe my feet with extra care when I went back inside the house.

I have no mirror so I have no idea how I look. Since my hair is short, it doesn't take long to dry and will stay fairly neat. The only way I can get along with my hair is to keep it short. It has always done as it pleases and if I let it get the least bit long, it is impossible; being short, it can't get too carried away. I flossed my teeth and got dressed. I put on a slip; no way would I wear one of those Sag Harbor skirts without one! Then a navy, floral print skirt, navy sleeveless top, my socks and sneaks.

They served Jane and me breakfast of tea, biscuits and eggs. I passed on the eggs and just had tea and biscuits. I sweetened the tea with my little Equal tablets. There is sugar but I like it sweet and when I use too much sugar I get aching joints so try to keep that at a reasonable level.

We were due at the sick bay at eight. Jane and I walked there. The sick bay is on the dirt road we traveled on yesterday. So we retraced the route we took last evening, walking along the highway to the dirt road, crossing the highway to the dirt road and continued walking along that. I was a little more observant of my surroundings this morning. There are homes on both sides of the highway but the ones across the road from us sit back farther from the road. There is a store on the corner where there are many people and several seem to be tending a table affair where they must have things for sale. Everyone, it appears, is watching us. The small children especially. Some of the little ones are brave and call out, "Muli bwanji?", then giggle when we answer them. There are several homes along the dirt road on the right as we walk towards the sick bay. The village seems to start behind the market. The homes are mud or clay with floors of the same. The windows have no glass or screens but I imagine have shutters, the same as my bedroom windows, that are closed at night. Most of the roofs are of thatch.

As Jane and I walked towards the sick bay we met several others of our group and we all walked together. The sick bay is a new building under construction. It is located about halfway between the school and the highway. The materials were donated by the Peace Corps to the village. The villagers agreed to provide the labor to build it. It is a moderate-sized brick building, concrete floor and corrugated metal roof. The windows are high from the ground and two doors are at the front, one at each end of the large main room. On the one end of the building is the large room and at the opposite end are two smaller rooms. This building is to be used as a clinic and the two small rooms are to have beds for patients. At this point the Peace Corps is going to use it for classes.

None of the head trainers is at the sick bay when we arrive, so we go to Chris's home in the village. Chris is the trainer general, head honcho, or whatever; chief co-ordinator is the word I want, of the trainees' training. There is a path through the high grass that either begins or ends, depending on where one is going, at the dirt road across from the sick bay. We have met some of the trainers by this time. They too were awaiting instructions from Chris. They seem to know their way around so we follow them along this path. As we walk along, I notice there is a network of paths leading in different directions. By this time, I am completely disoriented as to directions, so I just follow everyone else.

Lo and behold! We arrive at the home where Chris is staying and everyone else is there already or arriving. After everyone is there and settled, we have an organizational meeting of sorts. We are redivided into new language groups for one. I am still with Stella, but the group is now Tara, Nancy, George and me. After this meeting the language group decides to meet at the sick bay at three o'clock. The organizational meeting over, we are free to go. I decided to go back to the Nyasulus' to study my language. I started on the path we followed to get here. This was fine until I came to a fork in the path and took the wrong one. I should have arrived at the dirt road and I didn't. I panicked! I was lost in the tall grass! It reminded me of the time when as a small child I became lost in the corn field! There was no one around to ask directions and I couldn't have if someone had shown up. I couldn't speak the language! *Help*! I turned around and followed the path back, hoping all the time I wouldn't make another wrong turn. There were paths heading in various directions, to where I had no idea. I did make it back to Chris's. Crosby was there and I explained to him what had happened. He very kindly walked me back as far as the proper fork in the path and pointed me in the right direction. I then found the sick bay and from there my way back to the Nyasulus'. Had I remained on the path I originally took, I would have ended up at the highway eventually; just beyond the market by the dirt road. Well, I guess I can't expect myself to know everything at once!

I must carry my water bottles with me wherever I go. This morning Beatie filled them for me from a large urn in the pantry. The urn probably holds about five gallons of water. They keep a porcelain plate on the top as a cover, and a cup for dipping it out. All the drinking water is boiled. Since the water is boiled over an open fire it tastes smoky. I hope I acquire a taste for smoke water. If not, too bad; it's wet! Carrying the waist pack has become old, fast! I have decided to just carry one bottle as long as I'm not going anyplace far or staying long.

When I arrived back at the Nyasulus', I made a trip to the chim. I asked Mayi for a basin of water to keep on the table in my room so I can wash my hands without bothering someone each time. There is antiseptic soap in the medical kit. I place it by the basin and use it to wash my hands. My camp towel hangs over a piece of twine stretched between the two windows, to be used as a clothes line.

After washing my hands, I took my books to the verandah and studied language for a while. Jane uses the verandah as an office so there are chairs and a table. As a Peace Corps official, she has business to attend to. This is a delightful place for such activity. Everyone should have an air-conditioned office as this one! However, Jane is not here at present so I take advantage of her absence and use it for studying.

The concentration started to become tedious after a while and I thought I would lie down and let the words flow through my mind. Sometimes it helps to remember things I am trying to learn. Ha! The rot has set in already! I fell asleep.

It was around one o'clock when I woke up. My stomach was telling me to put something into it. I asked Mayi for some bread as I would need to eat before I left for class at the sick bay. I was so embarrassed! They didn't have any bread and she sent someone to the store for some. Then, just when the bread arrived, lunch was served. Chicken, nsima and greens. Plus, I made it to class on time.

The sick bay is still under construction and was not too pleasant inside. Instead of trying to work around the construction mess and workers inside, we found some shade under a small tree, some stray bricks and a unclaimed length of a small tree, about three or four inches in diameter. We tried making that into a bench by placing the ends on two stacks of bricks. It was a little wiggly and not long enough for all of us. I made another stack of bricks, about seven or eight inches from the ground and sat on that. My chitenji comes in handy for many things and sitting on it is one of them. Other than sitting so low for an extended period of time on a pile of bricks, being less than comfortable, I have dealt with worse... We had our language class with Stella in our open-air classroom.

After class, Tara and Nancy walked back to the Nyasulus' with me. They wanted to see where I was staying. The nicest home in the village. Word had gotten out. They both let me know how lucky I was. Nancy was dealing with rats in her home. Everyone, or almost everyone has grass mats under their foam mattresses and the termites were eating the during the night. They also eat the thatch in the roofs. No one might know they were eating the except they are noisy. I haven't heard them but apparently they go "a-a-a-a-a-a". One of the fellows has chickens in his room at night. Apparently his bambo did not tell his to close his shutters. Everyone is having problems but me. I'm wondering if perhaps I'm not having a true "Peace Corps experience".

Bambo and Mayi were most gracious and gave Tara and Nancy the grand tour. They were impressed and reminded me again how lucky I am. I knew it and agreed with them. Bambo gave each of them a soda. He offered me one too but I declined. Diet pop is almost non-existent in the village if not in the country. I try to avoid the sugar to keep from having painful joints. I have no reason to believe the sugar causes the painful joints, but it happens often enough that I avoid the sugar when I have a choice.

After Nancy and Tara had left, I began studying. I have to do this in the daylight as the candlelight is just not bright enough for much "eye use". I did write a letter to Dodi to give to Chris or Crosby. They mail the letters in Kasungu when they make trips for supplies or whatever. I need to practice speaking these sentences out loud but feel foolish talking to myself. I have some privacy but not enough to be talking out loud to myself. My window opens to the backyard where everyone is working or whatever. Everyone here is extremely kind and helpful, but I would hate to have them think they had taken in some kind of nut!

Tea is served around five thirty or six o'clock. I'll not make the same mistake I did yesterday and eat a lot at tea and not be able to eat dinner. I suppose, in retrospect, it was a good thing I did as I was so exhausted by dinnertime I may not have eaten had I been able...

Bambo and Mayi eat dinner with Jane and me. Jane is familiar with the country, language and customs. Fortunately, I have her to keep the conversation going and inform me as to what is what.

The Nyasulus have ten children. The youngest, Ishu, is ten years old and in the sixth form at school. They also have a set of twins, Henry and Wezi, who are in their last year of secondary school. Wezi, a daughter, is not in school at this point as she became sick and had to return home. After the eighth form school is no longer free and only qualified students whose parents can pay go on to higher grades. When they do, they attend school any from home.

The Nyasulus are retired; she a nurse and he a district health official. They retired to Mphoma village to farm. Mayi also cares for two children of another daughter who is going to teachers' school in Kasungu. Her name is Agnes and she is the mother of little Thandi. Thandi is four and is not feeling well this evening. She has an earache. Thandi is the little doll who was helping me with my medical kit. Beatie is a village girl who works for the Nyasulus.

The children do not sit at the table with us. The rest of the family eat out of doors, sitting on grass mats. I think it must be neat; having a picnic every evening...

The Nyasulus are Christians. They say that the villagers don't like religious proselytizers who attempt to force their beliefs on to them.

It gets dark early and lamp oil is precious so we don't stay up late visiting. The Peace Corps has given each of us candles and matches. When we do any reading or studying after six o'clock in the evening, it is by candlelight. It isn't completely dark but I close my shutter at dusk because of the insect visitors. With the candle lit, they fly into the flame and sizzle. So I hear the occasional "pssst" of fried mosquito or other flying insect. The mosquitoes have not been a problem here, so far. This is the winter or dry season. There was a little rain while we were in Lilongwe. It never lasted long and dried almost immediately. For some reason there were mosquitoes in Lilongwe but I haven't seen many here. It has been mostly sunny in both places. There are a few small fluffy white clouds, but we haven't been here long.

Day XV

Wednesday, May 1, 1996

I woke up to my trusty alarm clock going "ko-ko-li-li-ko!" I close my shutter at night to keep out the insects. I still don't have string or twine to tie up the netting. I guess it is low priority as I have mentioned it more than once. During the day, with the shutter open and the curtain pulled away from the window, insects fly in and usually fly right out again. Once in a while a fly or something will land but arm or hand motion will put it back into flight. Anyway, I opened the shutter a bit and looked out into the yard. Sure enough, Beatie was sweeping the yard with a short-handled broom affair that appeared to be bush branches without leaves. I had noticed a regular pattern of brush marks in the dirt on my early morning trips to the chim. Now I was able to see first-hand who made them and how.

I have made trips to the chim during the night but put it off until I get really uncomfortable. I put on my flip-flops, wrap my chitenji around me, tie it behind my neck, put the toilet paper under my arm, the flashlight in my hand and set off, trying to be very quiet. I have to turn the key in the lock of the back door, open it, then close it quietly behind me and step carefully into the yard and starlit night. The first night I did it I wasn't sure where I was going and almost wandered away! There was a fire burning near the goat shed and the night watchman was curled up on the ground, asleep. That was what confused me as I didn't expect to see anyone, awake or asleep, or a fire.

There are huge cockroaches in the chim at night; some three and four inches long. They run when I shine the light on them. No flies come roaring out at night; but then I don't shine the light down the hole. No use looking for trouble and waking them up. Placing the flashlight so I can see was a problem to be solved. By placing it in the shoe box with the beam aimed out the door seemed to work well and would also warn anyone else on a chim run the place was in use. The guys probably just find a dark corner outside somewhere and let it go. Mother Nature didn't make us girls that way. We have to squat. I learned as a small child many years ago that out on the ground doesn't always work so well for us. If there isn't someplace for it to go, the feet get wet! I wouldn't try something like that here anyway. My white skin glows in the dark...

One time when I made the chim run, the night watchman was sitting by the fire. I said, "Muli bwanji?" to him but he didn't answer me. I either made a cultural "faux pas" or he is hard of hearing. The stars are plentiful, bright and beautiful and I would like to stop and look at them. Unfortunately, standing about staring at the sky in the middle of the night in my nightshirt doesn't seem like a good idea; so I hurry, run my little excursion and back to my refuge under the covers.

I don't need to make a chim run at this point. After peeking out, I crawl back under the covers. I don't need to get up yet, so I won't. When I do get up, I let Beatie know I am awake; and when may I take my bath? She nods, and after a time lets me know the water is ready and the bathhouse is available. I think I am the third or fourth in line. Beatie and Wezi get all the water from the well by dropping a bucket on a rope into the water and pulling it up, hand over hand. Then the water is heated over a fire in the backyard.

This morning I take my water bottle to the bathhouse with me. That way I am able to rinse my mouth and toothbrush. Also the stuff was thin enough, it ran out the little drain hole. Dumping the water from the tub cleans it out fairly well.

We have both culture and language class at the sick bay. When we sit inside, I put my chitenji on the floor and sit on it. The concrete is still damp and cold and the chitenji gets rather wet after a while.

This seems to be settling into a routine. After dinner I was telling my village family about my American family in Chichewa. With much encouragement from Jane and everyone I managed to get through it. Everyone is so helpful. I guess I should give myself credit for what I can do. They seem to understand my Chichewa but I can't understand theirs!

Day XVI

Thursday, May 2, 1996

This morning was more of the same routine. The only difference was that I washed my clothes. George doesn't like the eight o'clock language bit, so we have moved it to nine. Wezi brought me a bucket of water and two empty ones. One for washing and two for rinsing. I have the small bottle of Woolite for soap. My underwear I hung on the little clothes line in my room but the socks, skirts and blouses I hung out on the backyard clothes line. All this before class! In Malawi one washes one's own undergarments and they are never hung where others might see them.

The laundry was finished and hung in time for me to walk to the sick bay for class and arrive on time. We sat outside on our bricks for class. I feel absolutely lost in the language. I have started making flash cards of the words, nouns and verbs, but putting them together is confusing to me. There are words that are used with different classes of nouns and we must use the right pronoun. "Ndi" is first person singular. "Mu" is second person. "Ti" is third person. "Li" means "is" or "are". "Ndili" is "I am", "muli" is "you are", "tili" means "he, she or it is". I guess it is a beginning; but I still can't understand what they are saying to me.

When one of the trainers says, "Mwaswera bwanji?" to me, my mind goes blank. It has happened more than once! They won't say, "Muli bwanji?" That is too easy! Stella is so sweet. She is trying to teach me and I am trying to learn. I keep reminding myself, if I don't learn it, I don't stay.

This afternoon we had a concerns meeting. We have been divided into four smaller groups and each group met with one of the trainers. Most of the concerns have been resolved at this point. Nancy's family got a cat to catch the rats. They may also be trapping them. It seems they caught one and wanted to show it to her. That, however, was not her idea of a trophy to be admired!

The termites have been foiled from eating the mats by putting plastic sheets under them and somehow Robert got rid of his chickens. I'm not sure how that happened but he probably closed the shutter on his window! I can imagine how he felt waking up with a bunch of chickens in his room…

I have a concern but I don't think I want to bring it up at the meeting. I have green diarrhea! Yuk! I feel okay so it is probably the diet. They don't worry about diarrhea. Just eat and keep yourself hydrated. In the States we would run for the Imodium. Here we run for the chim! It is probably all the greens I am eating. It may not be green, either. The toilet paper is blue; perhaps it is the color combination along with the poor lighting in the chim. I don't think I'll look the next time; I don't even know why I looked when I did. It doesn't make a difference and given a choice, I'd rather have that problem than constipation!

This afternoon after class, I copied some of my notes and tore the old ones into tiny pieces to throw on one of the fires which are always burning. Jane suggested the next time I not burn them but take them to the chim and put them in the shoe box. The Peace Corps keeps us supplied with toilet paper but it is a luxury here. As a matter of fact, we were advised never to offer someone our left hand. And, never, never use our left hand to reach into a community serving dish at the table. Water is always offered before meals, along with soap and a towel to wash hands. But still, never reach into a serving dish with the left hand. In some situations all food is eaten by everyone at the table from one dish. The Nyasulus don't or haven't served us that way; but it needs to be known in case we are in a situation where food is served in this manner.

The Peace Corps gave each of us a large flashlight, which is great. It is bright. Not only that, it has a loop on the bottom so it can be hung up. Now I can read and write without eye strain. I have been going through the Hypotears! I wrote a letter to George earlier and now I can study later with the light.

Today was Mefloquine day. I don't dare forget that!

Day XVII

Friday, May 3, 1996

I woke up at the usual time. I didn't sleep well but I think it may be the Mefloquine. I had another vividly colored dream. I think it was about women plowing fields with old-time plows being pulled by black and white cattle. The women were white but dressed in African clothing – chitenji. I think I was in America but can't be sure. Nor was I in the dream; I was just watching it. I was having other dreams but remember less of them. What I do remember doesn't make sense but seemed normal while I was dreaming it.

When I went to the chim I was still having the loose, I imagine, green. I feel great so won't worry about it. My digestive tract is probably responding to the diet change. The food is always quite tasty although I'm not sure what I am eating at times.

One day there was something with brown gravy that I had never seen before. Jane didn't know what it was either. It appeared to be part of an intestinal tract but the wall was thicker and the inside lining looked as nothing I had ever seen… The stuff was attached to the inside wall, whatever it was. Gut of the type sausage is made from is thinner. This was thick and gristly appearing. It was chewable and tasted okay. I ate some of it but have no idea what it was. Perhaps the making of green diarrhea in an old mazungu…

I bathed, shampooed, etc., and walked to the sick bay for class at nine. Another group had taken "our" spot by the brick piles. Workmen were busy inside the building and it was pretty messy. The doors are on now and it is dark and gloomy when the doors are closed.

We decided to walk back to the Nyasulus' and sit under the trees. There are a lot of shady areas in the front yard. That turned out to be a good idea. Bambo gave us some chairs to sit on so we didn't even need to sit on the ground. It was cool in the shade and a pleasant breeze was blowing. The "atmosphere" for learning was great. Now, if I could only learn it!

Everyone else in the group seems to be having similar problems. George however, appears to be doing better at talking to the villagers; I guess one might call it "conversational Chichewa" or "pigeon Chichewa"? When I ask how to say something and someone tells me, when I try to repeat it, my tongue doesn't work right.

The structured part of the language classes is to shorten next week and we are to get more individual instruction. Perhaps that will help. We are to be setting our own pace at this. It does seem to help when we go over the conversations in class. It gives me a chance to speak out loud and hear myself and others in a protected environment where I don't feel pressured.

We had culture class from two until four this afternoon. That was at the sick bay. Our culture group is a different mix than the language group. We have learned so much about family structure, village life, marriage practices, births, deaths, what is considered proper manners and what is considered improper manners; table manners, latrine manners; the list goes on and is endless. After all this, probably when I am on my own and caught in a given situation, I'll boo-boo!

Jane left this afternoon to go back to Lilongwe. I am going to miss her. She has been my liaison. Now I am going to have to do everything without prompting. I am so fortunate to have had her here. All the other trainees were on their own. All the homes where the trainees are living have someone who speaks English (Chimazungu) but it is still "do or die…" We must learn the language which means at least going halfway.

Beatie brought chips and bread with my tea. That is a lot to eat; I'll not eat dinner tonight. I can study my language.

Day XVIII

Saturday, May 4, 1996

This is my first day on my own. It started out as the rest of them. I am falling into a routine. I usually read my books, the *ODAT* and *Courage to Change*, then meditate for twenty or thirty minutes before I bathe, etc. I have absolutely no idea what I look like, how my hair looks, etc. I haven't looked into a mirror since I left Lilongwe. It seems as though I have been here forever and it hasn't been a week yet. It is so peaceful, calm, quiet and relaxing. The only thing I have to do is interact with the villagers, learn about the culture and structure of village society and learn the language. If I don't learn the language, I will only superficially learn the rest...

We had our language class on the verandah. Since Jane has gone we have taken over the "office". We are supposed to start at eight but George doesn't usually arrive before nine so once we start we don't take a break.

I did recopy my notes. I need to do the note recopying because when I take notes in class, my handwriting is undecipherable, even by me. If I wait too long to recopy them I sometimes forget what we were discussing and the notes are worthless. My short-term memory is short! I also made more flash cards. That seems to help to learn the vocabulary.

Wezi has been helping me with the language and I am so glad. I don't think Beatie speaks much English but the girls are both so kind. Wezi doesn't hesitate to correct me when I mispronounce something. Her English is excellent as is Ishu's and Agnes's. Agnes is going to school to become a teacher but the schools are on break now. The young women are almost always busy. They cook, clean, fetch water, do laundry, etc. Mayi runs a tight ship.

Every once in a while the girls will sing in the evening and I enjoy listening to them. They sit on mats in the backyard, eat dinner and visit. It is quiet family time. I'm usually reading or practicing my vocabulary but I can hear them singing with the shutter closed. I enjoy hearing them sing hymns in Chichewa. The melodies are familiar but of course the words are different.

Day XIX

Sunday, May 5, 1996

This day started out much as the others, except I didn't have anything scheduled. I decided to sit on the verandah and read the books in the medical kit. There are two books. One, written by Lucy and Neni, specifically for the Peace Corps volunteers and the other, *Where There Is No Doctor*, is for health care providers in remote areas. I had started reading the *Where There Is...* earlier and thought I would finish it or at least read for a while during the daylight hours while I had the chance.

Wezi came up and asked me if I was going to the picnic. No one had mentioned a picnic to me and I explained I didn't know about a picnic. Well, yes there was a picnic and Barbara, who is staying with her brother's family next door, and some others had gone to the sick bay to get a ride. I really ought to go. I didn't feel enthusiastic about a picnic and was anticipating a day of no class. Wezi, however, felt it was my official duty to go to this thing. I didn't want to create an international incident so gathered my water bottle, chitenji and ambled off to the sick bay.

When I arrived, there was no one there; not a soul was around. They had apparently left already. Wasn't that sad? It didn't exactly break my heart because I had been looking forward to a day of doing nothing. So I went back to the Nyasulus', the verandah and my books.

I hadn't been sitting long when who should drive up but one of the trainers, the driver and the P.C. vehicle. They wanted to borrow buckets from Bambo. Didn't I want to go to the picnic? It was on a mountain. Almost everyone else was already there. They had to go pick up Joyce and I should ride along. Well, what the heck? Let's go! I climbed into the back of the van.

Joyce is one of the trainers who teaches Chitumbuka. She lived quite a distance from the Nyasulus' with a Tumbuka family.

We went farther on the dirt road than I had been before; past the school, past a soccer field, then turned onto another dirt road before finally arriving at the home of Joyce's family.

While I waited in the van, Crosby and the driver went to fetch more water containers from Joyce's family. There were several small children standing outside the van looking in at me. A couple of the youngest were naked. They were wide-eyed and innocent as only small children can be.

I decided to try out my Chichewa, not thinking they were Tumbuka. "Ine ndine, Bea. Kodi dzina lanu ndani?" One brave little guy said, "Ine ndine, Sammy." At least I think he said his name was "Sammy". He was rather shy about speaking and I'm not sure it was "Sammy" but it sounded that way. That ended my ideas for conversation. I could have said "Mumachokera kuti a Sammy?" That probably would have had them in hysterical giggling. The question was, "Where do you come from, Sammy?" The child probably had been in that village and that house for his entire life! While I'm trying to think of some great question to ask them, the smallest of the group decided to "peek" at me through his fingers. That must be universal with little ones. I couldn't help myself responding to that and he gave me the most beautiful smile. It was better than the usual reaction of face hiding and wails from the tykes! Even Agnes's little one won't look at me. Perhaps this fellow felt brave. He was with older boys; no mother to hide behind…

At about this time Crosby, Joyce and the driver returned with more containers and we are ready to go. The driver heads the van toward the dirt road, I think. From this point I'm not sure where we are. We stop at another side road or path. Here we meet Alice and Mel, two of the trainers, and some of the trainees. They are filling buckets from a well. The buckets are filled and placed in the back of the van. We are off again. This time with more trainers, trainees and the full containers of water.

The road is a dirt one (what else?) and bumpy (what else?). The containers are full of water. Soon the containers are not so full of water and the van becomes a bit damp as well as does the merry group of passengers in the back of the van! Soon the driver turns right from the road and into what appears to be a corn field.

Actually it is the edge of a corn field. Then he stops, everyone gets out, takes a bucket or container of water and start to walk, one following the other. The trainees are doing as the trainers and placing the container on his or her head. I have a smaller pan with a handle and figure I may as well try it too. I hated to admit it, but it is easier carrying the weight on the head. I had to hold the pan on my head as I was afraid I would spill it if I attempted to balance it the same as the trainers were doing. I did fairly well until I came to the mountain and started up. One of the trainers came to my rescue and carried it the rest of the way up.

Meanwhile, I tried to get myself up this mountain, which was similar to a high steep hill. Probably no higher than some of those in south-eastern Michigan or north-eastern Ohio. Just straighter up with large smooth rocks jutting from the surface. There were thorny trees without leaves. I don't know whether the trees were dead or just leafless because it was winter. (Late autumn?) A question I would like to find the answer to. Perhaps after I have been here for a while I'll find someone to answer my questions. If my questions don't deal with language or culture, no one I ask seems to know the answer to them.

One of the volunteers, who was helping out while we were in Lilongwe, gave a great lecture on Malawi's history. He obviously had some great sources of information. I, however, did not get an opportunity to talk to him as there was so much else going on. Oh, well, I'll have time later.

I had to stop about halfway up to catch my breath. That surprised me; then I remembered the village is on a plateau. I'm not sure of the elevation, but I think it is greater than one thousand feet and I am going higher. One would think being in the village a week would acclimate me to the elevation. Perhaps. Though, this is just enough to do me in. After I stopped for a bit, I finished the ascent to where the activity vas.

There were three or four fires burning and pots of water on most of them. Some of the trainees were cleaning and cutting up vegetables and greens. And there were live chickens. They asked if I wanted to kill one of the chickens. I declined. They used knives to cut the heads off. That is slow and inefficient. If I have to kill one, I want a hatchet! None of this sawing back and forth with a knife that wouldn't cut butter!

Back in the olden days when I was a young kiddy, my father had a chopping block. This was actually a stump by the wood pile that had multiple uses of which beheading chickens was the least. Daddy, while holding the chicken firmly by the legs with one hand, would place its head on the stump, and with the hatchet in the other hand, quickly, with little fuss and ceremony, separate the chicken from its head. The chicken would flop around for a while until it was completely dead, but it was quick. Cleaning and gutting the chickens was something I wasn't interested in either. If I had to do it, I could. Let the young folks have the practice. I've been there; done that.

I found a small tree that had some leaves, providing a little shade, spread my chitenji on the ground and sat down. I was still a little winded and the shade, such as it was, plus a slight breeze, felt good. The view was great. Naturally, being up so high, visibility was miles, or seemed so. There were numerous similar mountains. These were separate from each other. Not as our mountain ranges but single, humongous projections from an otherwise flattish landscape. I had noticed them as we were riding the bus from Lilongwe. There are four or five visible from the village. From the mountain we were on more were visible. Also miles of pink-colored grass. I think the pink color is just the seed heads at the top of the grass. This is the high stuff they make thatch from and it isn't pink. Looking down, I could see footpaths, a road and a store that was on the road.

I did busy myself peeling sweet potatoes. I could do that and stay in the shade. The only problem was dealing with the peels. I was told to just throw them on the ground. They are biodegradable! They started attracting flies and one of the little devils bit me! It looked similar to what we used to call "sand flies". Those were biters too. I swatted at it but it got away. It did draw a little blood but I wiped that away and was more diligent about not allowing them to land on me.

Everyone was doing something. We had rice, macaroni, greens, assorted vegetables, chicken and sweet potatoes. Some of the fellows were eating the sweet potatoes raw! Finally, in due course, everything was cooked and we ate. The meal was quite good and everyone had plenty to eat. Then for dessert there was watermelon.

Clean-up was accomplished, the dishes washed in a large kettle of water boiling over one of the fires and things were packed to take back down the mountain.

Were we ready to go? No! We had a meeting! We were divided into four groups; our group had five persons in it. Some groups had more, some less. Each group was given an assignment. Ours was to talk to our "fathers" to get information and write a history of the village, something about the farming operation and do a time line using the facts we obtained.

We were sitting in the sun during the meeting. The bright light and the angle started to bother my eyes and I put on my sunglasses. They have prescription lenses but I hate them and only wear them when I am desperate. They did help the glare from the sun but I should have taken them off before I started down the mountain.

After the meeting, we each picked up something to carry and started down the mountain. I grabbed Bambo's bucket which was full of miscellaneous items. As soon as I hit a steep area I knew I was in trouble. I am not used to wearing the sunglasses except for driving and don't remember ever walking down steps while wearing them. The down focus is skewed. Wouldn't you know? I made a misstep and fell! I skinned my left shin and my right knee in a couple of places. Other than that I wasn't hurt. I bent Bambo's bucket all to heck and felt worse about that. Didn't split a seam, thank goodness!

But everyone was concerned. Mr. Chimzizi, our medical officer, asked several times if I was okay. I said, "Yes, thank you," and I was. I walked the rest of the way down without mishap. I took the glasses off... I wasn't as well off as I thought I was, however. My leg muscles were starting to rebel and tighten up from the exercise they weren't used to! Oh great! I knew what I was in for! The same thing happened last year when I took Bear down inside Seneca Cavern. I limped for two days! I was taken on the first van trip back to the village. Getting up into the van proved to be a challenge. Those hamstrings were in rebellion and I was so tired by this time, I didn't really feel I wanted to force them even one more time. I did and they responded. The ride back to the corner market where the driver left me off was forgettable. That is because by that time I was too numb to even try to think about how miserable I was.

I walked from the market to the Nyasulus'. My legs were really feeling funny by this time. I think this must have been worse than Seneca Cavern! That mountain must have been higher and steeper than it appeared. I think I was limping just because my legs felt so weird. I'm sure it wasn't from the fall. Mayi and Bambo both asked me if I was all right. I told them I was and went to my room after I made a trip to the chim.

As soon as I got to my room, I washed my hands, then washed the wounds on my knee and shin with boiled water and Hibclens. Then I put antibiotic ointment on them. After that I took my book, the one I had started reading this morning, went out onto the veranda and read until dark.

I must have looked worse than I felt because Barbara came over to see how I was. Then Mr. Chimzizi came to see me. He told me the Nyasulus were concerned. I guess they went over to get him. He lives with a family on the other side of the highway.

He brought his medical kit with him. I showed him the scrapes, told him what I had done and tried to reassure him I was essentially okay. He suggested I keep a clean dressing on them until they are healed. I guess he has to make out some kind of report. I also explained, I am an old lady and not used to climbing mountains. My legs were doing what out-of-condition legs do when expected to perform. I would be all right in a day or two. He seemed to accept that and left.

My legs will be screaming tomorrow! If the muscles are complaining today already, I can imagine what tomorrow will bring. We shall see. I'll try to stretch them a little before I go to bed. Ha! It may help.

Mayi brought me some delicious fried chicken and bread. They are so kind to me.

Day XX

Monday, May 6, 1996

Another beautiful day. We were to be at the sick bay by eight o'clock. We were scheduled to have CPR, First Aid and gamma globulin. Most of us were there by eight, the others were there by eight thirty. However, the crew from Lilongwe, who were to teach the classes and give us the shots, were not there. Bill Kernan, from way up north somewhere, arrived first. He was the dietician who lectured us on nutrition while we were at the Kalikuti. He made the two-day trip by bus. Bill had made some muffins in his iron oven and brought them along for us to sample. I think he wanted to let us know that we can feed ourselves well using primitive equipment. The muffins were good and it was thoughtful of him to bring them for us.

The trainers brought some games to pass the time while we waited for the instructors. The fellows were having quite a time with a game using tops and corn cobs. The tops were made from sticks, about four or five inches long and one-half to three-fourth inches in diameter; the sticks were whittled to a point on one end. The stick was inserted through a flat disc of about four inches in diameter. I couldn't tell for sure what substance the discs were. Each player had four half corn cobs. These were placed on end, one player on each side of the room. The object of the game was to knock down the opponent's corn cobs by sailing the top into as many as possible. This became a little wild. I, unfortunately, was sitting on the floor behind one of the players. Occasionally, I was hit by an out-of-control top. It was fun to watch and the flying tops were a minor discomfort! Some of the fellows became quite proficient after a few games.

There was another game, I think called "fuwa"; I may be mistaken about the name. I wasn't paying much attention to that one. It has a flat wood board with, I think, four parallel rows of holes.

The players use stones. I think the object of the game is to get all of one's opponent's stones. I'm not sure how this is done. It is a quiet game and the corn cob melee is more of a spectator sport. I, being the spectator!

Things finally were organized, sort of. We had a class with Bill, as the Lilongwe group was so late. Pat was to give us a lecture on safe sex; even brought bananas for a demonstration. They were so late, however, that she said she would return next week for the lecture; we could have the bananas to eat. We were not allowed the bananas though until we had had our gamma globulin! What a bummer... A 2 ml shot in the right hip! Ouch! After that one, the banana was a nice gesture.

I was late getting back from the sick bay – one o'clock. Dinner was waiting for me. Rice, beans and pigeon. Many of the people raise pigeons for food. It is quite good.

I made some more flash cards as they seem to help me learn the vocabulary. There is so much to learn. Wezi and Agnes were helping me for a while. I discovered that I could recognize the word in Chichewa and could give the English translation. But if I heard the English word, I had trouble coming up with the Chichewa.

One of the words is "chinangwa" which is cassava. I told Wezi I did not know what cassava was. I do know they eat the tops as greens but had no idea what it was. She went and got one to show me. It is a root, long, thin, tuberous with a skin I might compare to a sweet potato. They peel them and cook them. I haven't to my knowledge eaten one yet. Tomorrow I am to get up early for a cooking lesson.

I did get my laundry done this afternoon. Now I have damp underwear dripping water on the floor. The rest I hung outside on the clothes line. It doesn't take long to dry things outside because of the sun and the breeze. The socks sometimes take a little longer but the rest goes quickly.

My leg muscles are sore! What really kills me is using the chim! I can walk; a little stiff legged, but I can walk. Squatting however, is *agony*! Perhaps another day and it will go away. I have lots of company! Everyone I have talked to is complaining of the same thing!

Day XXI

Tuesday, May 7, 1996

This has been a quiet day. We had language class here from eight until twelve. I still feel lost although my vocabulary is getting larger. I don't understand sentence structure; what words are used with what nouns, for one thing. It depends on the class. I suppose at some point this will all gel but for now it is confusing. I think part of the problem is, I am trying to use English grammar rules for the Chichewa and can't seem to shake the mindset.

Wezi and Agnes have both been helping me. Mayi seems to be away as I haven't seen her. The daughters and Beatie are looking after me; giving me my meals, etc. Wezi gave me some fried bread which I dearly love. It is similar to French toast without milk mixed with the eggs. I think Wezi gives me things she likes when Mayi isn't around. Mayi sees to it that I have rice, beans or greens, etc. I don't get the fried bread often; probably as I turn down the eggs. My breakfast usually consists of bread and tea by my preference. They would give me eggs but I don't care for eggs much. A little goes a long way; preferably with something else such as coating on fried bread! Sometimes I put the dried milk into my tea as at my age I suppose I need the extra calcium.

This afternoon I walked to the sick bay for my individual instruction. Stella is so nice and answers all my questions but as for individual instruction? I don't know where to start. When I ask a question, the answer flies right over my head. We laugh but it rather scares me.

After I came back to the Nyasulus' I wrote letters and did the flash cards again. I looked at the language schedule guide and we are way behind where the trainers think we should be. We are supposed to be halfway through the book! I could kick myself. I just glanced at it when it was given to me. I should have checked that out more closely! We are to be setting our own schedules and

I have been depending on Stella to tell me what to do! I guess I had best start learning words and conversations ahead in the book… We should be able to ask travel questions, know directions, trade at the market and much, much more than we are.

Stella has us writing sentences which I do all right on. But writing sentences and speaking are two different things. And understanding when someone speaks to me? Not yet!

I have half a headache. I am flooding my eyes with Hypotears, which helps a little. I also have sores in my nose that I would dearly love to put some Neosporin on. They are up too high to reach with my finger and I don't have Q-tips. I didn't think to put some in my medical kit. Complaints! Complaints! Squatting in the chim is still an ordeal but better today than yesterday!

Day XXII

Wednesday, May 8, 1996

Morning routine was the same. Today, however, I washed my sheets and nightshirt. I had much help from Wezi and Agnes for that job. Bar soap and by hand. Wringing them out was a real trip! Well, it had to be done. My nightshirt was taking on a life of its own.

Language was from nine until noon. Chris stopped by to tell us that culture was cancelled and Jane was returning. I gave Chris the letters I had written to mail for me.

Agnes and Wezi were helping me with my language this afternoon when Jane arrived. Jane brought the mail with her from Lilongwe. I received a letter from Kimberly. Barbara, who has been writing many letters, many, many more than I have, received three letters. We were both so touched by getting mail that we were on the verge of tears. I never thought a letter could mean so much.

This afternoon I wrote letters. I answered Kimberly's letter. I also wrote one to Richard asking him to purchase more appropriate gifts for Mayi and Bambo. I thought I would be with a young family and think I should get them more age appropriate gifts. If he gets them as soon as he receives my letter and sends them to me, I should get them before I leave the village.

Day XXIII

Thursday, May 9, 1996

Bambo's nephew passed away sometime during the night. He apparently had been sick. He lives in the house next door, opposite the Nyasulus' from where their son lives. This family has been so co-operative and helpful to the Peace Corps. Lucy, the nurse, has been living with the nephew and his family, Barbara is living with their son and his family and Jane, when she is in the village, and I live with Mayi and Bambo.

I woke up sometime during the night to whispering conversation and people in and out, so I imagine that it happened around whatever time that was. I knew something was amiss but they didn't say anything to me. I was told later, when I got up.

My routine didn't change much. I had company at breakfast, Lucy and Jane. It was pleasant having company, although Lucy and Jane had things to discuss so I mostly listened. They courteously included me when they could.

Class met at the sick bay as Jane uses the verandah for her "office" while she is here. Besides they didn't think it would be in good taste for us to be next door having a class while there was a wake. The villagers started visiting next door early and there was a steady stream of people passing. There is a garden and some shrubs separating the two houses but the pathway is partly through the Nyasulus' yard. So, we were right there.

While we were in class, we were discussing if and when we should go to the wake and what to do if we did. Stella explained the procedures to us. The women go inside and sit quietly with the widow and the men, meaning George in our group, sit outside. Around ten o'clock Crosby came by and answered all our questions. He suggested we go to the wake at that time. After Crosby left, we walked back to the Nyasulus', followed the path to the house next door; the path we ladies took led into the backyard. George went around to the front of the house where the men were sitting. There were women preparing food in the backyard and one of them directed us to the back door. We filed in quietly. The house was crowded, filled with village women. Stella found us each a place to sit down. This was still painful for me as my leg muscles were still complaining when I stretched them and sitting on the ground was a stretch. But I did it. Most of the women were sitting quietly but the widow and several women who were near her were keening. It was spiritually moving. We sat there for about fifteen or twenty minutes when some more Peace Corps people arrived. We left as quietly as we had come in and walked back to the sick bay. No one had much to say.

I had company for lunch again. Sabina, Lucy and Jane. Mayi came into the dining room to go into her room. I went over and gave her a hug as she looked so sad. That was a faux pas. Malawians don't do that. Cultures crossing, I guess. She didn't seem to mind but, I guess, was surprised; and well mannered. The others explained, after she left, that it was not culturally correct. Only Mazungu do such things. Oh, well! It probably won't be my last boo-boo…

In the afternoon we had a large group meeting then divided up into smaller "concerns" groups and had another meeting. So, we spent most of the day at the sick bay. Jane left again after the meeting. She had to meet with some trainers to prepare for our camp week. We are all looking forward to that. The word around is that there are real toilets and showers! By that time I won't care about the toilets but they would have been more comfortable this week. Squatting is still a "pain"!

My eyes were burning and hurt so I didn't read or write letters after I returned to the Nyasulus'. I just moped around. Then I fell asleep to the singing and keening next door. It was a sad, haunting sound.

Day XXIV

Friday, May 10, 1996

Wow! What a night I put in! I woke up at around ten thirty as I had fallen asleep without making that last chim run. And I had to go! They always leave the key in the lock so I, and others I assume, can go out the back door to the chim during the night when necessary. The key was gone! It hadn't fallen to the floor so I was apparently locked in. I didn't want to wake anyone up so quietly suffered the agony of a full bladder.

I didn't hear the clock strike three or four so did get some sleep. When it got a little light I thought I would try again. Perhaps someone would be up. I found the key! Someone had placed it on the pantry shelf, the pantry being right by the back door. I let myself out and headed to the chim.

Who should I meet at the chim but Barbara! She had mentioned yesterday she had 4K stamps and needed 1K stamps as postage is 5K. I wasn't able at the time to offer a trade-off as circumstances didn't allow and Barbara is a butterfly. She is young, full of energy and has an amazing mind. But anyway, when I was in Lilongwe, purchasing stamps, they were out of everything except 1K stamps. I loaded up with 1K stamps. Unfortunately, since my envelopes were not large, I had to cover my letters with stamps. Here we are at five o'clock in the morning, discussing a stamp trade-off by the chim, in a remote village of Africa. Now here I am telling my grandchildren about it. Barbara will have to wait a few years before she tells her grandchildren unless she marries some old guy with a family in place... I did empty my bladder and felt much better.

Bambo and Mayi are away. The nephew was from another village and the custom is to be buried in the village of origin. They are traveling to the other village for the burial. The girls are looking after things and it is quiet.

Wezi fetched me some water so I could wash my clothes. Hooray for Woolite! Unfortunately, there was some soot on the pail somewhere and my clothes have black streaks! They come out with extra Woolite, so I'll work on the streaks the next time I do laundry. My white underwear is the only place it is noticeable and no one sees it but me. I was late for language class at the sick bay as I took too long doing laundry. I don't think anyone really cared.

We had no class this afternoon so I just hung out again. Studied my flash cards and grammar. The grammar I can't make head or tails of. And we are way behind what the competency schedule has mapped out for us. I'm really becoming concerned. I suppose I should be more philosophical and quit worrying about it. But I feel these people have great expectations from us and I personally would hate to let them down.

We are to have a little break this weekend. No planned activities. Shadreck was here at around three o'clock with the trainer evaluation. He is such a kind person and has the most beautiful smile.

This evening I wrote letters. I started while it was still light and continued until long after I lit the candle. I'm back to candlelight again. The batteries in the big flashlight didn't last long; of course I was using it a lot because it was bright. I only use my regular flashlight for trips to the chim at night. I don't want anything to happen to that. It is usually light enough from the moon and the stars to see basically where I am going but the chim is *dark*. I suppose I could use a candle if I had to... I keep my small flashlight under my pillow so I can always reach it. Sometimes if I wake up and wonder what time it is, I use it to look at my watch. Mostly it's for the night-time chim runs.

Several days ago the batteries died in the big number. I was wondering to my language group about how I could get more batteries. George mentioned they had them in the little store on the corner. I am not comfortable going there as there are always many people around and with my deficient language skills, I hesitated; George told me he would come with me as he wanted to get a soft drink. So, with a strong, young escort, I felt brave enough to venture to the store. The guys go there all the time. I haven't known any of the girls to go there without an escort although they may. But I went to the store to get batteries. While I was there, I thought I would ask them if they had any string. He didn't know what I was talking about and George couldn't make him understand either. Then I noticed a big spool of string that he used for tying around packages. I pointed to it and asked if he would sell me some. After he figured out what I wanted, he gave me a lot and didn't charge me for it.

I was actually happier with the string than the batteries. Now I could fasten the mosquito netting up. I not only had enough for that but George took what was left to use for a clothes line. I have learned to appreciate little things. I thought I did before, but some things really bring it home. Who would ever think they could be so elated over a couple of yards of string? The batteries didn't last long. Not as long as the original ones. As I said, I'm back to candlelight.

It is hard on the eyes. I have dry eyes and the constant reading in poor light seems to aggravate it. I guess I'm falling apart! I have sores inside my nose. I keep trying to put the polysporin ointment on them but they are high and no matter what I try nothing reaches them. I go to bed early. Can't say I'm not getting enough sleep!

Day XXV

Saturday, May 11,1996

Bambo and Mayi returned sometime during the night. I awakened to someone pounding on the door. I knew they were away and it frightened me as it didn't occur to me they were locked out. Wezi and Ishu were apparently sleeping soundly as only the young can sleep. I called out "Who's there?"

"Henry!" was the response.

I did a double take as he had been "Bambo" or "Mr. Nyasulu". The first name threw me. They were my "parents"! I got up quickly, unlocked the door and ducked back into my room. I didn't have time to wrap my chitenji around me. The nightshirt covered me from neck to ankles and has longish sleeves but still, I was in my nightshirt and didn't want anyone to see me. I was glad they were back.

I have been having a four-legged visitor during the night. I thought at first it was one of the kittens Agnes and Wezi allow to stay in the house at times. They come into my room to see me sometimes during the day when I am there. I discovered it was not the kitten. I had been leaving the waist pack on the table with the backpack. It has been easier to carry only the water bottle when I go to class, etc. The pack is heavy to lug around as I keep an assortment of personal items, such as comb, toothbrush, toothpaste, small hair brush, shampoo, Woolite, etc., in it. The shampoo and Woolite were together in a plastic sandwich bag. The toothbrush and paste were in another. When I took the shampoo out of the bag, I noticed little droppings! Uh, oh!

Perhaps the perfume in the shampoo or the Woolite had some appeal for a hungry critter. After I got cleaned up, I went to work on the bag. I found droppings in the bottom of the bag. The bag was cleaned out, the top zipped and hung on a nail. The backpack I keep zipped so it wasn't bothered. I'm glad it wasn't a little lady mouse who decided to set up housekeeping. That *would* have been a surprise!

Mayi has been involved caring for the sick nephew and then his death with all the arrangements. The young ladies are not as careful about crumbs, etc., when she is not around to remind them to tidy up. Mayi is an amazing person. She manages the place and keeps the young people busy doing all the things that must be done. She never raises her voice, but when she speaks, they listen. Since she has been otherwise occupied, things get done, but not with the same careful detail as when she is there.

I found the droppings yesterday and realized it wasn't the kitten. When I heard it again during the night, I sat up, turned on the flashlight and tried to see if I could see it. I couldn't. That worried me. I'm glad my parents are home again. That is one of the reasons.

Two of the Nyasulus' older daughters are here now too. They both teach school in Blantyre and are on break for a month. Their names are Carol and Charity. Both are kind, thoughtful and helpful. And I am in luck! They seem to understand what I don't understand. Carol started out by asking me about my family. I am supposed to be able to do this in Chichewa. She was patient, gave me more and better words to use and helped me use them correctly. I feel encouraged; she and Charity will be here for a while.

Day XXVI

Sunday, May 12, 1996

This has been an interesting day. The morning started out fairly routinely. Then Henry, Wezi's twin brother, walked into the backyard carrying a dead chicken which he showed to Mayi. Mayi looked at it sadly, shook her head and said, "Snake."

I heard that and gasped. "A poisonous snake? My God! What if it is out there crawling around when I go to the chimbudzi?"

She thought it was funny. " Don't worry, it is in the bushes."

Well, the chickens do wander around in the deep grass and the bushes. There really isn't any place a snake could hide in the yard as it is mostly packed dirt. But it could hide in the chim at night. I didn't say anything but I will sure be on the lookout!

After lunch, Barbara and I walked to the sick bay as there was going to be a program. The Nyasulus said they would come along later. We met others from the group as we walked and by the time we arrived there were many others, trainers and trainees. The van was going to take us to the soccer field where the program was to be held. A large number of us climbed into the van. It is a wonder how so many people can be packed into one of those vehicles! We started down the dirt road towards the school, then continued past the school building; much farther. We stopped at a group of homes to pick up some chairs. Apparently a Tumbuka headman lived there. I thought it was crowded before? We continued on our way. As we drove, we passed many walkers and some bicycle riders. A few of the trainees were walking; mostly the fellows.

We arrived at the soccer field and everyone climbed out. This soccer field was like none I had ever seen before. It was mowed to about a height of four or five inches. The grass was brownish, the ground bare in some places and there was stubble. The stubble was anywhere from one quarter inch to one half inch in diameter. As I'm walking through this, wearing shoes, the stubble is scratching my ankles. I comment on this and wonder out loud to Alice, one of the trainers, about how the children play soccer on this, with bare feet even! One of those stubble stalks would go through my foot if I weren't wearing shoes! Alice giggles and says, "Oh, Bea. We're used to it!" *Wow*!

It must be true. Many of the children play soccer without shoes. We had discussed that before. Adam, one of our group, shared that, when he was in high school, his family was host to some exchange students from Nigeria. They played soccer with bare feet. Adam felt if they could do it, he should be able to do so. He broke his foot!

This was the boys' soccer field. We had passed a soccer field closer to the school where the girls play. In Malawi the boys and girls don't play together. The sexes are carefully separated. Even married couples don't walk together. The man usually walks ahead. The woman walks behind with any children, often carrying a burden of some sort on her head. Men will also carry things on their head but only if walking alone.

We walked across the field to a small stand of trees at the edge where there was a little shade. Grass mats had been spread on the ground. This is where we seated ourselves. The few chairs that were there were reserved for the dignitaries; headmen, others in official positions and some male trainers (our leaders). Many people were standing and we formed a large circle – theater in the round?

Several of the men gave speeches in Chitumbuka. This so that the villagers could understand. Shadreck, one of our trainers, translated into English for us so we could understand. Shadreck speaks five languages, fluently. There were speeches throughout the program.

The villagers, mostly young people, put on skits and dances. The dances were similar to the ones they had done the day we arrived. Young men beat rhythms on the drums. The girls danced in a circle, wiggling their little derriere in the most unbelievable fashion! I can't believe they do that without dislocating their hips! Some of the trainers joined the circle of girls, much to the enjoyment of the trainees. Then the kwatcha and tambala started flying into the circle of dancers!

There were several skits. One was particularly funny. It was performed by the fellows. A couple were in drag. This can be hilarious and it was. The message was to show youngsters what happens to people who indulge in alcohol, drugs and promiscuous sex. The fellows in drag were prostitutes and one young man milked it for all it was worth. He was over six feet tall, thin, wore high heels, a red "slinky" dress, with purse, jewelry, the works. He minced around in a campy style, adding levity to the skit where the hero self-destructs due to choices he has made.

Another skit had both men and women interacting publicly. This was unusual as it is not much accepted in the village; men and women interacting publicly that is. The skit was on family planning and the need to get man involved in the process. There were also several children in this one.

One young student read a poem she had written. The cadence was pleasing, but wasn't translated so I didn't get much out of it. Another man, not so young in appearance, demonstrated a couple of traditional, home-made instruments. Those required a great deal of skill to play. Also the medicine men performed some dances.

The program was to demonstrate methods used to convey healthy choices for the young people. It was arranged by the villagers, performed by the villagers, and directed by the villagers; adults and children. The village leaders are trying to cope with widespread illiteracy in the villages. This especially among the women.

Education is free, provided by the government for grades one through eight. It is free but not compulsory. Many families do not see the need to educate girls as they are needed at home for work. It is a labor-intensive society; as was true in the United States not that many years ago. People have large families as the children are free labor. With the extremely high death rate for children under five, often they are unable to raise them to adulthood. The children are not unteachable; just untaught. Many don't – especially the girls – learn basic reading and writing. Most of the children, although unschooled, are able to speak at least two languages, often more.

More of the boys go to school, at least until the eighth

standard. Only the brightest and best students are educated beyond that level. The children who are schooled beyond that level must leave home and village and stay at the school, often a considerable distance from home. They only return home during breaks in the school year. The breaks last one month and the sessions last three.

Not only must the child be an excellent student, but unless they are exceptional the parents must pay tuition. Schooling is only free for the first eight years. Even if the parents are willing to pay tuition for a child, he or she is not accepted unless they are willing students.

The churches provide schooling for some. However, that is limited for a variety of reasons. Missionaries started the early schools. The missionaries were also the force behind the halting of the Portuguese and Arabic slave trade. Malawi was a major source of slaves as the people are generally friendly, peaceable and hard workers. Malawi has an ancient and extremely interesting history. However, this is off the subject, which was the program.

It was after five by the time I arrived back at the Nyasulus'. It was teatime, one of the most pleasant times of the day. Mayi started putting milk in my tea. It is delicious. It never occurred to me before. Sugar? Yes. Milk? No. I know people who put milk in their tea but it never sounded good to me. Well, it is good. I recommend it to anyone. Barbara informed me, she loads her tea with the powdered milk as it is about the only source of calcium. She is right. So I had tea with milk. An enjoyable way to wind up an enjoyable day.

That wasn't the end of it though. I read for a while; by candle-light of course. Then it was dinner time! Nsima and beans.

Day XXVII

Monday, May 13, 1996

The day was fairly routine. This morning we had class with Mr. Chimzizi. He and Lucy are the medical persons for our group. Lucy is the senior person and one or both of them are here in the village at all times. He lectured on diseases, fevers, etc. He went into details at great length. Much of what he discussed I already knew but the others might not. I am the only nurse in this group. Malawi has an excellent school of nursing. I have met some of the people affiliated with it and was impressed.

After the lectures we had more immunizations; rabies #3 and meningitis A/C. I have been fortunate; I haven't had reactions to any of the immunizations thus far. I can remember getting sick from all of them, smallpox, typhoid, etc., when I had them years ago. The only thing that encouraged me at the time was, had I developed the diseases, I would have been sicker, if that was possible, or worse, died...

I really didn't feel great this morning and lay down and took a nap after lunch. I felt somewhat better when I woke up. Then Carol gave me an interesting lesson before I left for class at the sick bay.

Nsima is the staple of the Malawian diet. It is made from maize. The maize is white rather than the yellow of our corn. The farmers are harvesting at this time. It is being dealt with by the women mostly. Mayi had the teenaged boys build a storage area of grass. This was built inside the fence and appeared almost as part of the fence. The ears of corn are stored in the husks in this storehouse.

The process, after the corn is picked, continues with the removal of the husk from the ear. Then the corn is shelled from the cob and placed in a large basin or one of the large flat baskets that are used later for winnowing. When a large quantity of the corn is shelled, it is ready for the next step.

This involves a mortar and pestle. The mortar is made from a tree section and is from twelve to eighteen inches in diameter; and probably about that high. The tree section is hollowed out in much the same manner as the drums. The sides are about an inch or an inch and a half thick; the bark has been removed. What we have here is a large wood bowl with sides perpendicular to the bottom.

The pestles are small trees or large straight branches of a tree. The size and length of the pestles can vary. Some are three or four inches in diameter and perhaps five or more feet long. Others might be a couple of inches in diameter and shorter. The pestles are shaped so they are larger at the bottom and tapered towards the top, similar to a baseball bat.

Next comes the hard part. The kernels of maize are placed in the mortar, water is added, the women take the pestles and pound corn until the shells break and the soft inside is exposed. One woman alone may do this or perhaps two or three may if there are enough people available. The more women pounding, the more co-ordinated it becomes. As one pestle goes down another comes up, similar to piston action in an automobile engine.

The ladies were showing us how this was done and allowed us to try. I'm getting out of shape! After the episode with my legs from the mountain climb, I hesitated to give more than four or five whacks! The pestles are small trees and heavy! Barbara was more gung-ho. She was able to keep up with the young women. I'm afraid I was outclassed! Barbara's "mother" was pounding with little Stella on her back in a chitenji. It was comical as every time she would hammer down with the pestle, Stella grunted as though she was doing the work!

After the shells are crushed and broken, the contents of the mortar are emptied into the large, flat, round winnowing basket. This basket is at least twenty-four inches in diameter. The winnowing begins. This is done by taking the basket in both hands and, with a twist of the wrist and a quick lift of the arms, tossing the contents of the basket into the air a little. This allows the shells or "ga-ga" to fly out of the basket. It is a tricky process. With practice, I was able to do it, but poorly. Barbara as usual became quite adept.

Grass mats are spread out on the ground in the backyard. The winnowed maize or "mphala" is placed in the sun to dry. It looks as though it is white flour; but they are not finished with it yet. After the mphala is dried, it is put into bags. A woman will put the bag of mphala on her head and carry it to the mill. I did not have the opportunity to see this part of the process. Only observed as village women walked, carrying the heavy bags on their head in a seemingly effortless balancing act. I say "seemingly" effortless as it is as "effortless" as ballet is. The dancers make it appear that way. Considerable physical endurance is required in both instances.

After it is ground well at the mill it becomes "ofa". Ofa is stored in large closely woven baskets. These baskets are at least twenty-four inches in diameter and also that deep. The baskets are covered with lids, also closely woven. The baskets of ofa are kept in the storeroom next to the cooking room or "kitchen" for want of a better word. There is probably a name for it; I just don't know it. My education at this point has many gaps.

After class at the sick bay, I read and studied until bedtime.

Day XXVIII

Tuesday, May 14, 1996

Today has been mostly a language day. The group session on the verandah in the morning and individual session in the afternoon. We have been in training for four weeks. The group language is most confusing. According to the competency list we are way behind. I have been trying to go ahead, learning vocabulary in lessons beyond where we are. I still can't put words together to mean anything! Stella answers my questions but I get the feeling they aren't the right questions; I don't feel any breakthrough.

I really feel rotten today. Perhaps a reaction to the immunizations yesterday. And I was just thinking how lucky that I hadn't had any reactions! Oh, well. Today I'm just going through the motions.

Day XXIX

Wednesday, May 15, 1996

Today was another interesting day. Last night was not so great. I didn't feel good yesterday and went to bed and slept after an early chim run. I woke up with a headache and neck ache and thought, "Oh, God, I have meningitis!" I had been congratulating myself that I hadn't reacted to any of my immunizations; now this! It wasn't, meningitis that is, but I lay awake, uncomfortable for a while, then fell asleep again. When I woke up this morning I felt great.

Well, not exactly great, but good. I'm half constipated; it is probably something I did or didn't eat. I imagine I notice it simply because most of the time it is just the opposite. I don't think I have had what for me is a normal bowel movement since I left Ohio. That would indicate it is diet... What a gas! Perhaps they will feed me beans. That will get things moving.

The group I am in that was organized the day of the mountain picnic had a meeting at the sick bay at nine thirty. We are supposed to be doing a history time line affair but haven't done much with it. It is due to be turned in on Saturday. We were given the assignment on Sunday 5, ten days ago. We, or rather Shadreck, made up a list of questions to ask our "fathers". Bambo has not lived in the village for very long and most of the questions he couldn't answer. He did say he would ask the headman who has lived in the village forever. He is old. He appears older than I am but it is hard to tell.

Bambo did ask. The headman visits Bambo occasionally. I have met him. He stopped at the Nyasulus' when I first arrived to greet me. He doesn't speak English and I don't speak Chichewa so after "Muli bwanji?" and a handshake the conversation was up to Jane and the Nyasulus. Actually, I think his visit was more an official visit as Jane was staying at the Nyasulus' also. She is next to Vyrle in authority and is accorded much deference by everyone here.

The answer he gave to the questions was surprising, I think. One of the questions was, "What important events have happened in the village?"

One answer was, "Several years ago nine goats got loose, wandered into the road and were killed by cars and trucks." That would be, seriously, a major loss! Another event was during the years of the drought. The government sent maize to the village so they would have food. Someone stole the maize! Nine goats and a load of corn may not seem a great deal in our overfed society. However, there it is! An interesting thing to me is the fact that so far I have seen exactly one obese person in this country! Obesity is so common in our country, no one thinks anything of seeing obese people. I did a double take when I saw him. The only one.

All in all, comparing information, Dan had the best answers from his bambo. I had much the same answers as he did but his were more complete. Mr. Nyasulu has not lived in the village for long and he had to get the answers from others. Dan's bambo felt the building of the school was the most important event. At the meeting Suzanne said she would work on the time line. We have just three days to get it completed and turned in. Paper is the big problem.

This afternoon was the dedication of the sick bay. It is completed and looks good. The windows are high up and have decorative concrete blocks in them. The doors are on, the walls painted and it is ready for use by the village. The one large room can be used for clinics when the medical people are in the village for under-five immunizations, etc.

All the trainers, trainees, headmen and villagers were at the dedication. There were speeches that were translated. From English to Chichewa and Chitumbuka and then from Chichewa and Chitumbuka to English. Our Peace Corps director, Vyrle Owens, and his wife were there, plus several others from the Lilongwe headquarters. Refreshments were served; real soft drinks!

The mail came with the visitors from Lilongwe and I received a letter from Mary. It was postmarked April 26. Three weeks for mail. It is so great to get letters. It is also disappointing not to get any when the mail is brought. Whenever someone comes from Lilongwe they bring the mail. This may be once or twice a week.

I have a word list that Tara gave me to copy. It has a lot of useful terms and translations plus a lot of medical terms and phrases we'll need to know. I am copying it and am to give it to Christa when I finish with it. It is in Chichewa and I thought Christa was learning Chitumbuka but it does not matter. I'm just glad to get the list and we can't learn too much. Someone got the list from one of the volunteers and it has been making the rounds. More things to study!

Day XXX

Thursday, May 16, 1996

My morning routine is pretty well established. This morning though I did my laundry. I had to. I was out of clean clothes; unmentionables. I got that out of the way. I wore one pair of socks two days. I have been lucky as I haven't developed any skin problems, specifically athlete's foot. I usually, at least at home, back in another life, bleached my socks just to prevent such an occurrence. I was concerned about washing them by hand in cold water yet. So far no problem. I wear sneakers and expected my feet to sweat but none of my concerns have materialized.

We had culture class with Lucy which was neat. She hasn't taught us any classes until today. Lucy is a quiet, level-headed person and I was impressed with the class. We talked about what young women are expected to know and be able to do before marriage and weddings. We aren't talking sex here! It's work, hard work. The bride had better be able to pound maize and cook nsima or she is in trouble!

After class some of the trainees were playing fuwa, a game with stones on a board with four rows of eight holes or depressions. Each of outside rows has two stones (I think) per hole. I'm trying to explain a game I know nothing about... But the idea of the game is to get all of your opponent's stones by a series of maneuvers. It isn't easy and the game can go on and on with skillful players. Someone started showing Adam how to play and he went through several players by the time I left the sick bay. The other day when the fellows were playing with the tops, I didn't think the board game was very interesting to watch; however, it also can be a spectator sport. I don't know if anyone ever won the game at the sick bay or not.

My family asked me several times if I liked fish. I, thinking of filet of sole or something similar and not the fly-covered specimens at the market, said, "Yes, I like nsomba." I should have guessed by the look I got each time I said I liked fish that perhaps I should have thought that one out more carefully! Today I had nsomba; that with rice and beans. The fish was fried, whole, and was all of two inches long! I tried to eat it but decided, "Sindik-onda nsomba. Iyayi!" I supposed I could have chomped them a couple of times and swallowed. But I left them; three of them on my plate. I'll never tell anyone I like fish again! Lake Erie perch they ain't!

This afternoon I read and worked on flash cards for awhile; in fact I spent most of the afternoon in my room. Oh, I wrote letters too.

I made a chim run around dusk and stopped and watched Charity and Barbara play fuwa. Barbara is getting very good. It is fun to watch people play, but I haven't tried to play it yet. It became dark while I stood there and watched. I don't know how they could see what they were doing. Now *that* was a dumb comment; I was watching them, wasn't I? When I did come in I had to use the flashlight so I could see to light my candle.

Day XXXI

Friday, May 17, 1996

We had language on the verandah this morning. It is pleasant out there. Still, much more so than at the sick bay. Here we have chairs and the table; Jane's office. However, she isn't here, therefore it is our school room. Stella leaves the easel with the large paper and black markers for writing. Wezi and Agnes look at the things we are supposed to be learning and shake their heads. They speak it so I guess we seem backward.

I did learn something helpful I didn't learn in class. I don't know if Stella told us or not. If she did it didn't sink in. The letters "l" and "r" may be pronounced interchangeably. Wezi pronounces the "l" as "r" and I was having trouble understanding things she said that I should have. Had she used the "l" sound perhaps I may have understood.

One day I asked if dinner was ready. She answered, "Dakrani pongono." I didn't understand what she said. "Pongono" means "slowly" but I didn't understand "dakrani"; I couldn't translate. I asked her to repeat it. She gave me a look only an exasperated teenager can give, and repeated it. I still didn't understand. Finally, she said, "Wait a while."

Oh! "Daklani!" – "You wait." "Pongono" – "a while." I knew that word but that wasn't what she said. Later someone explained about the letters. Now I listen more carefully but still find it difficult, because of the mindset, I guess. Wezi has been pretty patient with me, but I suppose any teacher becomes discouraged with a dull student!

My eyes have been bothering me for several days. Today it is worse, I imagine from trying to read and study by candlelight. I guess when Abraham Lincoln did it as a child, his eyes were more adaptable. Or, he didn't have "dry eyes" as I do. My eyes didn't bother me at first but lately they have been driving me nuts! I have been using the Hypotears almost in excess. There are Visene drops in the medical kit but those are not good for dry eyes. I think I'll rest my eyes and see if that helps.

We had a trip logistics meeting at the sick bay this afternoon. We'll be leaving for camp on Sunday instead of Monday. We will need our books, sleeping bag, mosquito netting; actually everything we need here except the bedding. It is exciting, although I like it here.

After I returned from the meeting I decided not to read, write or use my eyes for anything except looking around. I asked if there was anything I could do. Mayi put me to work shelling corn. That was fun. I haven't done that since I was a child and then I never stayed at it long.

Dad had a corn sheller. It was an apparatus where the corn was dropped into the top, a large wheel on the side with a handle to turn, and the shelled corn came out a chute affair into a basket and the cobs into another. As a child it was high entertainment to be allowed to drop the corn into the top while someone was turning the wheel, and watch the shelled corn and the cobs be shaken along; the corn dropping through a screen and into one container and the cobs in another.

I wasn't supposed to play with the equipment, but kids being kids, and I was at one point, if the corn crib wasn't locked, often would go in and play with the wheel on the thing; turning it with gay abandon. I guess I thought it was pretty neat. Sounds dumb now but when I was little I didn't think so.

One day when I was "helping" my father by dropping the corn into the top, I decided I was big enough to be allowed to turn the wheel. Dad didn't know I did it when he wasn't around. I begged and pleaded. Any dummy could turn the wheel. I guess he figured it wasn't worth making an issue over and he was right there.

To make a long story short, I broke my arm and Dad had the guilts. He was concerned about that for years. Every time the subject of "Babe's" broken arm came up, he always said, "I shouldn't have let her do it. And I was standing right there!" Actually, it hurt him more than it did me. After the initial wailing like a banshee and being a holy terror at the hospital when it was set, it didn't bother me much. Nor did it slow me down.

The corn sheller at the Nyasulus' was not an invention of man. It was the one made by the creator that I carry around with me every day. My two hands. Mayi gave me a basket of maize. I sat down by the back side of the house and started working kernels off the cob. My fingers started getting sore after a time. Agnes then demonstrated how I could use a cob to accomplish the same thing. That worked great. I was able to shell more corn faster. The only problem was I developed a blister and sore hands.

I had bread and cabbage for dinner and went to bed as soon as it got dark.

Day XXXII

Saturday, May 18, 1996

I'm a mess. I have a headache and burning eyeballs, the former probably being caused by the latter. I didn't sleep well last night. I wasn't restless, just wakeful. Usually if I react to the Mefloquine I do it on Thursday night. But it may have been a delayed reaction. I heard the clock strike eleven, twelve, one, two, three and four. I didn't want to get up this morning, but I did.

I don't want to read anything either but duty calls. I washed, brushed, ate, blisters band-aided and was on the verandah by eight. Everyone was late this morning. George usually comes wandering in around nine but Nancy and Tara are always prompt.

I waited until eight forty-five and decided I had my wires crossed and we were to have class at the sick bay. I picked up my books, chitenji, water bottle and started walking to the sick bay. I was almost halfway there when I met Nancy. She told me Stella had gone to Lilongwe and had given her a letter to read as an assignment.

We turned around and walked back to the Nyasulus'. We met Tara on the way and George arrived on schedule; his schedule. As soon as we were assembled and settled, Nancy opened the letter and read it. Apparently, she had to go back to work as she said goodbye in the letter. She cited personal reasons for leaving. It seemed strange, unless a family member was sick or something. She apparently had to leave in a hurry. Nancy, Tara, George and I talked for a while then went our separate ways. Nancy had laundry to do, Tara and George thought they would go climb a mountain and I... I guess I was angry. This is just great! Here we are, way behind in our competencies and now the teacher leaves! I wandered into the backyard.

Wezi was busy with chores. I asked her if there was anything I could do. She said, "Yes. You can wash the dishes." Okay! Let's do it! She placed two pans of cold water, a piece of cloth that was once part of a sack and a bar of soap on the grassy area in the backyard. Soap the cloth, scrub the dishes, rinse them in the second pan of water and, after rinsing, place them to dry on the drying rack. Thoughts going through my mind – We aren't going to dip these things into boiling water? We are going to leave them outside on this thing? Uh, oh!

There is a small patch of grass in the backyard, perhaps three meters square. Beyond that, by the fence is a frame made of sticks fastened together, probably with grass. The frame is about four to four and a half feet high, extending back along the fence about two yards or meters. There is a grid of sticks fastened to the frame. It is on this grid that I place the dishes face down to dry.

I do as I'm told. Had I known the logistics of the dish washing three weeks ago, I would have been on the first plane back to Toledo! As it is, I'm fine, haven't been sick except for the eyeballs and they don't count. I don't think about it. After I got over being "grossed out", it was funny!

Getting enough water is a problem. The Nyasulus have a well. The women obtain water from it by dropping a bucket on a rope down into the water and hauling it back up, hand over hand. The rope is made by tying strips of cloth together. The cloth appears to be burlap but feels similar to coarse linen. I suspect, but don't know, that it is made from flax and probably is a coarse linen. The dishcloth was of the same material.

All the bath water, cooking water and laundry water is obtained this way. After it is lifted from the well, if the water needs to be heated, as for bathing, the bucket is placed over the fire to heat. The ladies are up before daylight doing all this. My foray at the well was less than successful. Besides almost losing my glasses down the well, I was not very tidy about extracting the bucket after filling it. One of the young ladies came to my rescue. I rather suspect she didn't want her rope tangled up. There is an art to this, you see. Barbara was quite adept at the water bit. She often made trips to the well for her "mother". It was not unusual to see her walking by with a bucket of water balanced on her head. The village women have my admiration; to carry it that way and not spill a drop!

Today I did no reading. Instead, I shelled corn. I started out with bandaids over my blisters. However, they w ere more bother than they were worth. I ditched them. Using the cob to push the kernels off doesn't cause the same type of wear on the skin; it wasn't much different with or without the bandaids,

The chickens hang around where we are shelling the corn. I throw them the defective and deformed kernels. The little devils don't want the defective ones; they go for the good ones that fly out and miss the basket. I discovered I lose fewer kernels by shelling into my skirt which I made into a receptacle between my knees. When that gets full, I stand up and pour the kernels into the basket. Thandi helps me at times but she is little, gets tired and wanders off. When I find a small ear, I give it to her and tell her it is a "Thandi" ear. This seems to tickle her as I always get a delightful smile from her.

This has been a quiet day. My eyes aren't bothering me so much; I'm still not going to read tonight.

Day XXXIII

Sunday, May 19, 1996

This is going to be an exciting day, and sad too. The trainees are going to leave for a week at Kasungu National Park. Agnes, Wezi, Carol and Charity will all be gone when I return. Agnes and Wezi to school; Carol and Charity are going to their homes and also to school, but as teachers.

I had fried potatoes and bread for breakfast plus the usual tea. At around eleven o'clock Mayi wanted me to eat lunch. There was no way I could eat again. She had the fried bread and insisted I eat. When I told her I just couldn't, she told me I should take it with me as I would probably be hungry before we arrive at the park. I deferred to her superior judgment and put the bread into my bottle bag. I filled one bottle with tea and the second with water.

I had help carrying my gear to the sick bay where we waited for the bus. When the bus arrived we had the luggage shuffle. Most of the things were tied onto the top of the bus. However, much was also inside with us. I had my medical kit and the waist pack with the carefully wrapped fried bread and the bottles of liquid refreshment. The seats were no larger on this bus than the one we arrived on. I sat near the back and next to a window. The bus was crowed and we were excited.

As the bus left the sick bay our families and other villagers were there to see us off and wave goodbye; we of course were waving back. Then down the familiar dirt road, a right turn onto the highway, past the Nyasulus' and I was away from the familiar; on a different side of the now familiar mountain and with twenty-seven kilometers to Kasungu.

The driver turned the bus left off the highway onto a road that took us to Kasungu. I was on the opposite side of the bus from the District Hospital where I will be assigned so was unable to see much as we drove past it. Kasungu doesn't appear to be a very large city. We stopped at a P.T.C. store and were allowed to go in and shop. Wow!

It was a small supermarket. I was so pleased to see it! The market in Lilongwe was intimidating and I have been concerned about my poor language skills. Seeing a real supermarket is reassuring. I think I'll be able to handle it!

I bought some soap, laundry and toilet, some clothes pins and a cold Coke. I was even able to deal with the kwatcha and tambala! They charged me for the Coke bottle. I didn't really want to carry it with me; I poured the Coke into the water bottle. Now I had Coke in one and tea in the other; no smoke water for me! Back to the bus and off we go to *adventure*!

I'm really lost now. We drove through city streets for a while and then back to dirt roads again. This is a "Cedar Point" special! We left Kasungu about twelve thirty. The first half hour of the trip, on paved roads, was okay. But then, for approximately two hours that seemed twenty, we were bounced, jostled, pitched, thrown about and generally misused. The scenery, when I could look at it, was fabulous. Outside Kasungu, before the going got rough, we passed one of the homes of ex-president Banda. It was the most impressive home I have seen thus far in Malawi. But then I haven't seen much of Malawi yet.

We passed signs saying "Nature Preserve", but still continued on. At last we came to gates where we had to stop while Chris and Crosby spoke with uniformed guards or rangers. Through the gates! Surely we were at our destination? No! It wasn't so. On and on we went. Some sections of the road seem to have been leveled a little and were a trifle smoother. We continued onward. By this time we could be in Zambia but the bus driver showed no sign of stopping.

Finally, we turn off the road and into... our camp! This consists of a large clearing with several cottages, a shelter house or pavilion affair, restrooms, a large fireplace and a sheltered building for cooking. We are surrounded on all sides by bush! But what is really great, we have Jane and several volunteers waiting to greet us.

We unload our gear and pick cottages. The cottages are round, rather large and have conical, clipped thatched roofs. Inside are beds, six in ours and a couple of them are bunked. Tara, Barbara, Danielle, Alice and I are in the same cottage. On each of the bunks we find a large bottle of orange drink, candy, writing paper, and pens; gifts from the volunteers. They have also provided twine so we can put up our mosquito netting.

Danielle decided to use one of the bunked beds, the easier to fasten the corners of the net. In the process of trying to tie it, the top bunk fell on her. Fortunately, she wasn't injured. The accident unnerved her and it no longer seemed a safe place to sleep. She and Barbara decided they would rather sleep out under the pavilion. They took their sleeping bags and mosquito netting out there for sleeping and just left their gear in the cottage. For night-time that left Tara, Alice and me in the cottage.

After the gear was stowed and things settled we decided to look around. Tara and I thought we would explore a little and started to walk along the road we came in on. It was a pleasant walk. We passed some elephant droppings and were foolishly, secretly, hoping to see the elephants that had left them. We were probably a quarter of a mile from the camp when a busload of people came along. They had passed us away then stopped and backed up. The guide on the bus told us we must go back to our camp. It was not safe for us to be out wandering around. Disappointed, we turned around and went back to camp.

Dinner that evening was abundant; chicken, cold slaw, beans, tomatoes and potatoes. Jane had brought her cook from Lilongwe and he outdid himself. I hadn't eaten since the fried potatoes at breakfast and ate a lot.

The restrooms were real modern facilities compared to what we had in the village; flush toilets and showers. Also anopheles mosquitoes. The little devils do sit with their ends straight up in the air!

I often wondered, many years ago, how one could tell if one was being bitten by an anopheles. All mosquitoes put their ends up in the air when they bite. Now I know! They can't be missed. And they are small. Probably the very ones that bit me in Lilongwe; although, in Lilongwe I wasn't really looking at the mosquitoes other than to notice they were small and plentiful.

Day XXXIV

Monday, May 20, 1996

Well, last night was interesting. I went to bed early as I was tired. I then woke up at about one o'clock with an urgent need. I thought perhaps if I ignored it, it would go away. It didn't. I lay there almost an hour. Finally I thought, What the heck? Perhaps I could quietly get up and not awaken everyone. I quietly undid the mosquito netting so I could put my feet out, surreptitiously turned on the flashlight and aimed the beam towards the floor so that I could find my flip-flops. As soon as I turned on the light, I discovered that Tara and Alice were both awake!

Alice had to "go" too, so I had company. Two flashlights are better than one. When we arrived at the chim there was a candle burning so we had more light. There were also two stalls so we didn't even need to take turns. We did our duty, washed our hands and went back to the cottage.

We were all awake and hungry. I remembered my fried bread. Alice and I each had a piece of that. Tara had some bread and peanut butter and ate that. I was surprised that, after eating a huge meal before retiring last evening, I was hungry. But I was. The fried bread tasted great at that point! After that little adventure, I fell asleep again.

I woke up in the morning when Barbara and Danielle came in to get their supplies to shower. All right! We can take showers! Cold showers but showers. However, after my experience with the cold water, slow drains and no place to hang things, I was almost wishing I was back in the village. The cold water was refreshing but I didn't feel clean.

We couldn't drink the tap water. They kept boiled water for us at the cook house. I put iodine tablets into that. I continued using the boiled water for brushing my teeth too. There were anopheles mosquitoes in the chim. They sat on the walls and fixtures but didn't fly much during the day. So far, no mosquito bites.

This morning Nancy, Tara, George and I had our first language lesson with our new teacher, Shadreck. He is great. I feel as though I can learn something now. It was a difference in teaching methods, I guess. Stella was a sweet person, but I suppose an inexperienced teacher. I had nothing to compare her with. We are way behind and will be playing catch-up for weeks. Now, however, I feel good about the language. The rest of the group is angry about it. I was angry too the other day when we read her letter, but I am over it now. Talking with some of the others from different language groups, I can tell how far behind we are. I didn't much have of an opportunity to talk to the others before camp. I knew from reading the competency lists, but thought perhaps they were setting high goals. No, they weren't. However, if we don't pass the tests at the end of training, they will allow us tutors. It isn't so discouraging now and I don't feel so pressured.

We had more immunizations before lunch. I don't need the hepatitis B as I had the series several years ago. I did take the tetanus shot though. I had a tetanus shot when I had taken the first hep B, but no record of it so took it again.

This afternoon I did my laundry. There is a clothes line behind the shelter house. I was able to hang my skirts and socks there. We used the twine, stretched between the beams, for a clothes line inside to hang underwear. The cottage is damp so it will take a while for the things to dry.

The whole group had fun and games in the early afternoon. There is a soccer field or just a large cleared area on the other side of the trees and brush, etc., that surround the camp. I'm not sure of directions here, but I think it is east of the camp. In the other direction, or what I think is west, the trees and brush go on forever; it is full of wild animals – the direction Tara and I started walking yesterday. Beyond the soccer field is a road that leads right, from the road we arrived on yesterday. There are homes or a small village on the far side of that road. These homes are where some park employees live with their families.

After being led by one ruse or another, the group went from the camp, through the trees, grass, etc., into the large field. I was unaware it was there. When Tara and I took our stroll, we turned right on the road instead of left. Had we turned left, we would have found the field and the village.

Our leaders started us off on games. In the first game we were caught by lions, became lions and tried to catch non-lions, hence turning everyone into lions; the last person caught was the winner. I was caught immediately which meant I had to catch one of the young people. Ha! The only thing I caught was a rapid and wildly erratic heartbeat and an overwhelming muscle weakness. This induced me to sit in the shade and watch everyone else become lions. I think my leg muscles are not going to allow me to abuse them the way I did going up the mountain...

My walking since I arrived in Malawi has been walking to and from the sick bay. The trips to the chim don't count. I can't believe I am this out of shape in four weeks! How disillusioning. I watched the others for a while, then took the road back to camp where no one was; they were all playing games I couldn't participate in; bummer. I studied.

Around four o'clock a huge safari vehicle appeared. This is the ultimate topless "Jeep". It actually was a Land Rover but as a Toledoan I think it resembles a Jeep. This was a fifteen-passenger number with a spotter's seat on the front fender. Who wants to go look for wild animals? It was raining a little but not too bad at this point. Alice, Rose, Joyce, Tana, Bill, Adam, Dan, John, the two Mikes (trainer and trainee) and I volunteer to go. Also there was the driver and the guide. Off we went in the rain, into the bush!

Did we see any elephants? No. Did we see any lions? No. We saw a zebra, a warthog, some wildebeest and some impala. Mostly trees, tall grass, birds and an assortment of vegetation. The guide didn't want it to be a total loss so he gave us a lecture on elephants and the vegetation. Elephants have several sets of teeth. They die of starvation when the last set of teeth wear out; they are unable to eat enough to sustain life. The so-called elephant graveyards are just places where the old elephants can find young tender vegetation. This is where they succumb to starvation and die.

The elephant is almost always walking. Sometimes they will stop for a while and lean against a tree, rest and start walking again. He told us of the fantastic amount of water they drink, forage they consume and the weight of their refuse! The guide was a veritable gold mine of information!

He also told us about the different types of plants, identified many, stopped so we could look at them. He explained that, many years ago, the British moved all the villagers out of the area because of the tsetse flies. The encephalitis or sleeping sickness, caused by the fly, was incurable and many of the villagers died because of it. The tsetse fly has been almost eradicated now. He pointed out traps that were placed in the bush. These use yak urine as bait. At one time the traps would be full but now there are few flies in them.

We rode around until after dark, then went back to camp. We were all rather damp from the rain. Sometimes it came down hard and sometimes it stopped, but we were damp. It also got chilly after the sun went down. Our dinner was served when we returned. Actually, they didn't wait for us. The folks who remained in camp had already eaten. There was a nice fire burning in the fire pit. I sat there with the others until I warmed up and dried off, then went to bed.

Day XXXV

Tuesday, May 21, 1996

I slept really well last night. I woke up once around one o'clock and went right back to sleep. This morning I decided to wait until afternoon to take a shower. Not only is the line long in the morning but the water becomes deep when everyone is showering. The drains don't work very well.

For breakfast I had cooked rice. I made some warm milk with hot water and powdered milk, then added a little sugar. I poured some of the milk over the rice, ate that, then drank the rest of the milk. I had forgotten how much I enjoy warm, sweetened milk.

The language is getting better. It seems to make more sense. I'm not sure if it is the difference in teachers or I have finally made the breakthrough. I have a long way to go but I can see a pattern. Shadreck makes sense when he tells about using certain words with the nouns, depending on the class. Stella explained some of this and what she said agrees with what Shadreck is telling us but, for some reason, now it makes sense. I think I just hit the point where the dawn breaks.

I hung some of the things I dare to outside in hopes it will dry. The things hanging inside are taking much time to dry. My bras got dry but the cotton stuff, no. It is still raining off and on. After I hung my socks on the line, the sky opened up and soaked them again. I could hang everything inside the cottage. However, it is warm and if it would stop raining long enough the things would dry.

The shower still filled with water when I took mine. I just hate standing in dank water even if it is my own dankness! I don't feel clean. Then trying to dry my feet is the pits. I waited until I got back to the cottage to do it. I am spoiled. I had better get over it!

Lunch was vegetarian. Potatoes, mixed vegetables with green

peppers and cabbage with onions. There is plenty to eat. After lunch was more fun and games.

I am sitting everything out. I have absolutely no stamina. It is a bummer. I was hopeful that this camp week would give me an opportunity to get some exercise and now I can't handle it! I don't even have the oomph to walk around the camp. My heart starts thumping and my muscles say, "Leave us alone! We can't and we won't." It is weird. They have never done this to me before. Maybe it is the iodine I'm putting in the water but I doubt it. That would send me into high gear, not low.

Anyway, I'm just going through the motions.

Day XXXVI

Wednesday, May 22, 1996

This morning we had three hours of language. We need it. I feel as though I would like to go off by myself somewhere and just try to digest it for a while. It makes so much sense while Shadreck is explaining it; then when I try to apply it I'm right back where I started. Well, not that far back, but I lose a lot. I must be patient. I can do this.

We were without water a large part of the day. I was able to do the rest of my laundry and brush my teeth twice but then the water was shut off. I didn't bathe! Egad! I hope the sun stays out long enough to dry the clothes.

More fun and games this afternoon. I sort of half participated. I am a real flat tire. This is such a disappointment. I had been looking forward to this week and I'm not even participating!

Our cottage was to cook the evening meal so we had that to do. We were to have pasta and Barbara was the pasta cook. The rest of us cut up vegetables and other food prep. Jane's cook did the meat. It turned out fairly well; we had lots of pasta.

This evening Adam brought his guitar over to our cottage and gave us a concert. He is quite a talented young man. He has his degree in public health. All these young people are multi-talented. I think it is great that at this point in their lives they are volunteering two years. Probably all their peers are working and making mega-bucks! This is a great experience; even at my age!

Day XXXVII

Thursday, May 23, 1996

Another bum night. All that wonderful pasta and I end up with indigestion! It wasn't the pasta, it was the other stuff. I took a couple of Mylanta tablets before I went to bed. At about four o'clock I woke up with a headache and stomach cramps. That was the beginning of diarrhea and several trips to the chim. I was able to go to sleep again and woke up late; seven o'clock. More cramps, diarrhea and the headache. I ate some toast and warm milk for breakfast, took a Tylenol and started to feel better.

More language. It is better for me but we are no way near competency. It is sad; most of the other groups are way ahead of us. No wonder Wezi thought I was backward!

In the afternoon we had a class on diversity which was interesting. I am more and more impressed with the young people who are in training with me. The volunteers who are acting as trainers here are also quite impressive.

I think the Peace Corps is the greatest idea. The money spent by our government on foreign aid is best spent right here and in similar countries on the Peace Corps. Anything else just goes to line the pockets of officials. The Peace Corps volunteers work with the people, possibly showing them how to do things. However, it must be something acceptable by the people that can be done by them. This ensures that the project can be continued after the volunteer leaves the country. Otherwise it serves no useful purpose.

I had another short bout of diarrhea this afternoon. I feel good, though; no headache, nausea or whatever. I guess I ate something that didn't agree with me. Or I had better start placing two iodine tablets into my drinking water.

I lucked out this afternoon and was allowed to take a second safari. This one was better. We saw two elephants. The first was a young bull that was walking through the bush parallel to the road we were on. That was scary in a way. He wasn't far from where we were and there was the thought that perhaps he might turn and charge the vehicle! He didn't. I have seen elephants in the zoo. This was different. He was in his natural habitat and the sound of his crashing through the trees was just a little unnerving...

The driver slowed the vehicle so that the elephant got ahead of us and crossed the road, then walked toward a lake on that side of the road. We passed him after he was across the road and halfway to the lake. Then we saw the second elephant. Wow! That was great.

The weather was sunny and warm and the animals were more visible than the other day. The day we took the safari in the rain the guide told us that the animals like to stay dry too and go deep into the forest where there is more shelter.

We also saw hippos. They sound similar to pigs! The hippos were in the lake. The driver stopped the vehicle so that we could get out and walk a bit towards the water so as to see them better. The guide warned us to get out of the way if a hippo should come along heading for the water. They run in a straight line for the water and would run us down if we were between them and the water. Fortunately, none did and we were able to watch them for a while.

This was a longer safari than the one in the rain. It was also through a different part of the park. We were able to see several herds of wildebeest and other such animals. After dark the guide turned on the spotlight but we were unable to see any more animals. He told us to look for eyes. We saw insects reflecting in the light but no eyes.

It was a late dinner again and more fireside comfort and warming. What was a bum night turned into a great day.

Day XXXVIII

Friday, May 24, 1996

This has been a slow day; cold shower, the whole bit. I am starting to get cracked skin between my toes. Great! Athlete's foot! There is cream in the medical kit so I slathered some between the toes and hoped for the best. I did more laundry. Since it stopped raining the clothes get dry rather quickly. My underwear, however, is always hanging in the cottage.

Today we had our mock language test. I know I didn't pass it. At least now I have an idea how the test will go. Lucy gave me the test and was very patient. If I don't pass the real test that we get at the end of the training, I will be allowed a tutor for a while. It is imperative I learn the language. Otherwise I won't be able to communicate with the villagers. I do feel a lot better about the whole thing now.

One of the volunteers gave a language session for anyone who was interested. It was a good thing to attend. She explained sentence structure. I wish I had known that even a couple of weeks ago. We are learning what adjectives to use with what nouns but not how to put them together. Now I want to go someplace and practice. Subject – tense – object – verb.

It is hot and I sat out the fun and games. I just don't know why I am so tired. I did go to the soccer field to watch a game that was organized between the Peace Corps trainers and trainees and the villagers. Some of the villagers wore shoes but some of the young boys did not. The Peace Corps team was made up of adults but the village team had some boys who didn't appear to be more than ten or eleven years old. The villagers are good. I didn't stay to watch the whole game. The final score was four–two. The villagers won!

Around four thirty the van arrived to take us to the lodge for a last night barbecue. I was on the first load. I hate to admit this but

I was hardly able to lift myself into the van. It is not really that high, but I need to pull myself up by grabbing on to something. Something is not right. Perhaps it is the altitude or the heat. It was still warm when we left the camp and I didn't think to take a jacket.

The lodge was heaven; real toilets, hot and cold water, paper towels. The gardens are beautiful. The lake lovely, placid, rippleless. The sky perfect. What can I say? One of those things or places you look at then attempt to absorb it all because you know you'll never see it again in just that way. This is where the trainers are staying. Next year I want to be a trainer!

A small group of us walked down to the lake, hoping to see more hippos. The ones we saw yesterday were on the other side of the lake. The rumor has it they were around here. We did not see any.

We walked back to the lodge where the others were gathering. There was a bar on the verandah and people were starting to get comfortable. I bought a Coke. Two in one week! I had had one on Sunday; now this! Then I found a comfortable seat and started talking with some of the trainers. By this time it was starting to become dusk and the mosquitoes found my bare arms. That was when I began to rue having left my jacket at the camp. No matter; I took my Mefloquine yesterday and had my yellow fever vaccine while still in D.C. I'll not worry. The bites I got in Lilongwe didn't itch much so I shouldn't even have that annoyance. Just swat when I see one. If I manage to kill one, it'll be one less mosquito to produce more little mosquitoes.

Everyone was enjoying this immensely. As it became more dark, the stars were bright and highly visible. A couple of trainers and I left the verandah and found seats by one of the several fires that were burning on the grounds near the main building. This helped alleviate the mosquito problem. The smoke helped keep them away, I think. At least, after we sat down near the fire, I didn't notice the mosquitoes.

Others came and joined us and we had a small congenial group gathered. Sometimes it happens when people are together, the mood meshes into something unforgettable. Something shared, pleasant and unspeakable. Quiet serenity. It was that type of thing; magical and enchanting. Probably the fire…

As we sat there, people not from our group would come and sit for a while then move on. There were quite a few tourists staying at the lodge. Finally, they told us it was time to eat. Eat we did. There was such a variety of food! And so much! I ate some roast lamb. I haven't eaten lamb in years. It was good but so was everything I ate.

We all took our plates back to our seats by the fire and enjoyed our meal there. Park employees continued to add wood to the fire. We didn't even need to bother with that. There was no hurry nor need to do a thing; just enjoy the moment. Time had stopped…

But all things come to an end. We finished eating and enjoyed the beauty, peace and tranquility of where we were. But the powers that be know how to end things. They quit piling wood on the fire. Then there was no reason to tarry. The workers wanted to get their work done and go home! We carried our dishes to the room where the dish washers were at work and joined the others who were congregating on the verandah. Some of the trainers brought cassettes and a boom box. The music and dancing started!

Several of us were ready to call it a night. The drivers, however, had instructions; no trips back to the camp until ten thirty. We stayed and partied. I can stand in a circle and clap my hands to the music. That is what I did. I'll not pass this way again, therefore will make the most of the experience. I wish I had even a fraction of the energy that was thrashing and bobbing around on the dance floor. You couldn't pay me to be young again, but oh, for just a wee bit of that zip and go. I don't think I would use it for dancing, but I sure wish I had it!

True to his word, around ten thirty, the driver took the first load of revelers back to camp. I was on that trip. By that time I am so weary it surprises me how one foot goes before the other. I just hope the young folks settle down and go to bed. I'll probably not know if they do or don't. It doesn't make any difference to me as long as they don't wake me up.

Wednesday night, the night I was sick, therefore I don't know how I missed it, but there was a "warthog" running around the camp, making a lot of noise. Barbara and Danielle had been sleeping in the shelter since Sunday when we had arrived. Kim apparently decided to join them out there. Kim woke up and was frightened while the thing was racing around the camp making fierce noises. Barbara said she heard it but went right back to sleep. Danielle slept through the whole episode. Alice said she heard it knock over a bucket. The ladies were in a panic about the event. Eventually, the two young men confessed it was they who did the dastardly deed. The volunteers had made some large animal silhouettes and hung them in the shelter. The fellows took one of those down, concealed themselves behind it and tried to scare the sleepers in the shelter. They only partly succeeded there but managed to frighten almost everyone else.

Day XXXIX

Saturday, May 25, 1996

It was almost eleven thirty before I got to bed last night; then I didn't sleep that well. Probably too much excitement. Or perhaps the Mefloquine. I was awake by six, cold showered, etc., by seven and pretty much packed to go.

I had left my clothes hanging on the clothes line last night. I may end up taking wet clothing back to the village. I'll leave the damp stuff hanging until it's time to go, then I'll pack it.

My breakfast consisted of milk toast. After last night's feasting, I think milk toast is appropriate. It tasted good. I brushed my teeth and checked the clothes line. Everything is packable except the nightshirt and some socks. I left them on the line and packed the rest. The bus is late. We are supposed to be back in the village by lunch.

I am excited about getting back to the village. The dynamics though will be different. Wezi will be in school. Carol was leaving on Wednesday for Blantyre. She too will be gone. Also one of the technical trainers may be staying at the Nyasulus'. But still, it will be good to be back.

The morning passed slowly. Eleven forty-five and still no bus. We are all waiting around, reading, writing, playing games. Everything is packed, ready to go. They were not planning to feed us lunch here and it is time for lunch. The powers that be scavenged up some cookies and peanut butter. Oh, great! Migraine city! I haven't had peanuts or peanut butter for years. All I need is to be vomiting and in agony on the three-hour trip. Well, it may not hit me until I'm back in the village. That is all there is to eat. Perhaps just a little peanut butter won't hurt.

I ate a little peanut butter on a cookie and will wait to see what if anything, happens. I then ate four cookies. In any case I won't starve; I'm not fond of the hunger headaches which I have from not stoking my overfed body with calories. If I ignore them they go away after a while, but I'm not good company for myself or anyone else when I have one. I filled my water bottles early as there would no longer be the ever-present boiled water after the kitchen was shut down, post breakfast.

After lunch I had the most foul-smelling bowel movement and was partially constipated. This is absolutely gross! I don't think it is from anything I ate last night but it could be, I guess. It was wicked! The worst part of it was I couldn't get rid of the smell. I must have gotten a little on my finger when I wiped as my *hand* also seemed to stink! I washed my hands well; I always do. Twice even, with Giesha soap which is perfumed. The smell remained. That used to happen years ago, before we had gloves to wear and Palmolive detergent to wash our hands with, when cleaning up an incontinent patient. The antiseptic soap often didn't cut it and we were left to deal with the residual odor. Now here I am in the middle of nowhere with stinky hands or hand!

That isn't the worst! Now I know I stink! I sat on the step of the cottage to write and the little gnats found me. How depressing! I hope it wears off soon as I feel sorry for the others when we get on the bus...

The bus! Someone went to the lodge to call the bus driver to find out when he would arrive. We were to be out of the camp by twelve and it was nearing one. It seems the bus was still in Lilongwe with a flat tire and the driver hadn't been able to get it repaired yet.

Crosby had been dispatched earlier to go into Kasungu to try to obtain transportation for us. Around one o'clock when Crosby hadn't returned, it was decided to start taking us back in the van. A bunch of us sardined into the van and started down the road. We just brought our medical kits and drinking water. The rest was left. The driver was not too happy about spending the rest of his day driving. This would have happened as it is at least a five-hour round trip. This would be the first of several.

We had been riding for about twenty minutes, were still in the park, when who should we meet but Crosby and a bus! Amidst the protest of all his passengers, Alison turned the van around to go back to the camp.

This proved to be a bit of serendipity. We hadn't gone far when someone spotted a whole herd of elephants! Alison stopped the van so we could watch them. Some of the passengers got out, the better to observe the large, gray mass in motion. I have such a deal getting in and out of the van that I stayed put. I could see fine where I was sitting. Another great experience.

Back to camp, then, following the bus. As we had stopped to watch the elephants, the gear was already being loaded onto the top of the bus when we arrived back in camp. Everyone was helping get the stuff stowed. Then we boarded the bus and were off. I was sitting in the middle of the bus so seemed more stable than the ride into the park. Although, it seemed the driver was driving too fast for the condition of the road.

The folks in the back of the bus were really getting bounced and someone yelled to the driver to slow down. The driver was either drunk or nuts. He began talking loudly and angrily, probably in Chichewa, gesticulating with both hands, at the same time. The bus, meanwhile, was moving rapidly along this bumpy, rutted road, with no hands on the steering wheel!

Chris and Crosby moved forward and attempted to calm the man down while the passengers were ready to mutiny. Half of them were calling out for him to slow down or stop. Our lives were at risk. Nothing stopped the man. We were bouncing along, out in the middle of nowhere with a crazy man at the wheel. Even Lucy tried to reason with the man.

Then it happened. A piece of luggage fell from atop the bus. He had to stop. Everyone got off the bus and refused to get back on unless he would drive more slowly and more carefully. He was adamant. He was in a hurry. He apparently had to be in Lilongwe by nightfall and if he didn't go fast, he wouldn't get there!

We were all standing in the middle of the road, refusing to get back on the bus. We were miles from anything. This man was willing to leave us there. Chris and Crosby, bless them, convinced the man he should drive carefully as far as Kasungu and leave us there. They would find another driver to take us the rest of the way to Mphoma village. The driver was as good as his word. He kept his hands on the wheel, drove at a moderate speed and delivered us safely to Kasungu.

We unloaded all our belongings and piled them next to a store by a vacant lot. I guess we were the entertainment for the afternoon. A busload of Mazungu, being left in a vacant lot with all sorts of neat stuff! We attracted an audience. We stood around for a while. I and others of the group went into the store and bought cookies, etc. This was a cookie day! Our lunch wasn't substantial.

Finally, our fearless leaders arrived with a bus and a driver. The gear was reloaded, the passengers reboarded and we were off. Hooray! This driver was nice. Of course, by this time we were riding on paved roads and could make pretty good time. Around five thirty or five forty-five, we arrived at the sick bay. Ishu was there and helped me with my belongings. I was so glad to see him and appreciated the help with the gear. I have all I can do to lift that backpack!

I was so happy to be back at the Nyasulus'! Mayi gave me some tea with milk. I think tea with milk is the Malawian chicken soup. It has healing properties! I had bread with my tea. I was absolutely exhausted and went to bed at six thirty.

I was also delighted; Carol was still there. Also her husband. She had become sick during the week and didn't return home. He came to find out why she hadn't come home as scheduled. Not having telephones can be an inconvenience. He came all the way from Blantyre. She said she was much better today.

Day XL

Sunday, May 26, 1996

I got up about six thirty and by seven thirty I was bathed, brushed, etc. I know I stank yesterday. Carol asked me if I wanted to take a bath last evening. I wanted to but said, "No," as I was so tired all I really wanted was to go to bed. This morning I feel better and I feel *clean*. Still tired but clean.

Today we met our technical trainers and got started on that. No language today but we will be busy for the next couple of weeks. Otherwise things are pretty routine. I'm still tired and went to bed early.

Day XLI

Monday, May 27, 1996

More routine. We just had one hour of language and heaven knows it isn't enough. We were to met at the sick bay at nine. The group from Lilongwe was supposed to be there but was not. We waited. Anna gave, us a short class but she wasn't scheduled for today. Breston talked a little about the cold chain. That is the method they use to ensure the potency of vaccines, etc. He will talk more on that later. It had to have been close to noon before Pat arrived with the bananas again. This time we put condoms on the bananas before we got to eat them. The Peace Corps isn't going to take any chances the trainees don't know what they are doing. I'm going along for the ride on this one…

The Peace Corps is strict on pregnancy. No babies are allowed to be born on foreign soil. If women get pregnant, they come home; either to terminate or deliver. The first time is excused, the second is cause for termination from the Peace Corps. For fellows, in case of paternity they are immediately terminated from the Peace Corps and responsible for support of the child until age eighteen.

The Lilongwe group brought in the mail. I received letters from Dodi and Millie postmarked May 8. Still no word from me. Dodi said she called Woody and he told her the mail would be slow, sporadic or both. I'm sure by this time the letters are arriving. I am surprised I haven't heard from Katie although I know she is busy.

Day XLII

Tuesday, May 28, 1996

I was up and bathed at the usual time and had time to answer my two letters. I must be at the sick bay by eight for classes. We are now divided into groups according to our assignments, agriculture, HIV counselors and child survival officers, as our duties will be different.

They are pouring information on us! I have a zillion handouts to read and study besides lecture notes. I'll never remember it all. It will probably all jell at some point so I'll just keep plugging away!

I tire easily and don't much feel like doing anything. Even studying is a chore.

Day XLIII

Wednesday, May 29, 1996

I had a miserable night. Was queasy and didn't sleep well. Since I take my Mefloquine tomorrow I can't blame this on that! I have been tired all day but went to classes, took notes, etc.

I started to feel better around mid-morning. In the afternoon we made some field trips. We went to another part of the village I was unaware existed. There appear to be several small villages or groups of families clustered around the core that is formed by the market, the sick bay and the school.

To go to this place we traveled by Peace Corps vehicle, along M-1, which is the main road. We passed the Nyasulus' house and a couple of others then turned left onto another dirt road, not as good as the one the sick bay is on. We traveled toward the mountain located behind the Nyasulus' house; not the one we had the picnic on. This was a very bumpy road. I guess I can say I was on the road less traveled. The driver may have been driving 2 mph and it was still rough. It seemed as though we were riding for a long time but probably weren't.

Finally, we arrived at a row of neat homes and gardens. The driver stopped at the first house. It looked similar to the Nyasulus'; brick with a corrugated metal roof. We were introduced to the owner who was probably a headman, but was not introduced as such. He was dressed in a gray business suit and I remember seeing him at various functions. He was a distinguished appearing gentleman.

He was the owner of a building that Bambo Doloni, the environmental officer from Kasungu, wanted us to inspect. A V.I.P. or Ventilated Improved Pit. A V.I.P. is a latrine built in a manner that they were encouraging the villagers to build. This was built in a similar manner as other enclosed latrines with three important differences.

First, it had a large, about seven or eight inch, pipe leading from the pit, up the back of the building, to the top. The pipe had a screen on the top. Second, it had a closable door. And third, it had a tight-fitting roof.

This is a method of keeping the insect population down. The door is kept shut when it is not in use. The only light for the flies and other insects in the pit is at the top of the screened pipe. The flies, etc., go towards the light, are trapped by the screen, die and fall back into the pit.

We were also shown an open pit. This was a deep hole that had criss-crossed sticks woven over the top to stand on while using the pit. One would need to be more agile than me to use that one! I could see myself when a toad or whatever jumped out at me! I would be in the pit with the rest of the refuse! They had an open well in this area of the village. The pit must be at least twenty meters from the water source.

The trip back was as slow as the trip over. As we were driving slowly along, a runner caught up with us and passed us! I was really too exhausted to walk over there if we had had to. I had all I could do to climb into the back of the van! It was quite a distance. One of the trainees had been assigned to a family in that part of the village originally but it was such a long walk that she asked to be moved closer.

I had all the walking I could handle later. We also stopped at a store that was across from the store on the corner of M-1 and our dirt road. Mr. Doloni wanted to show us a pump the owner had made to get water from his well. It was a basic pump scientifically, but had to be pumped from the top, similar to operating an old time butter churn. This was a deep closed well, meaning it had a cover. The Nyasulus have this type of well; however, the water is obtained by dropping a bucket on a rope.

After this we walked through the village to another neat brick house. This is where a village T.B.A. lived. A T.B.A. is a traditional birth assistant. This lady was also a T.H. or traditional healer.

The village T.B.A. is usually an older woman who has given birth and is a respected member of the village community. The health authorities encourage these women to attend classes on childbirth. This way they learn about methods of preventing infection, hemorrhage and other complications of childbirth. Also proper cord care such as not putting feces and dirt on the cord. This, unfortunately, is not an uncommon practice and frequently causes tetanus in newborns. They are also taught to recognize potential birthing problems that can better be resolved in a hospital or clinic.

This particular lady had been to the classes. She had a special small house she used for birthing. It had two rooms: one for family members and one for the birthing mother. The birthing room had a pallet bed, a small incubator-type warmer for the baby, plus instruments she might need for cutting and tying the cord.

As a T.H. she also did traditional medicine or acted as a "medicine woman". She told us she had a "dream" that told her to do this. The villagers have a lot of faith in her abilities. (I think my Mayi could be a T.H. She is a nurse and has a calming effect. I have faith in her!)

Mr. Doloni was encouraging. He told me, after I confided my lack of language skills, "We will teach you Chichewa!" I believe him! It will happen!

After all this I went back to the Nyasulus', went to bed and went to sleep.

Day XLIV

Thursday, May 30, 1996

I feel a little better today but wish this exhaustion would go away. I go to class and sleep. This morning I took my temperature just for the heck of it. It was 99.4°F. Low grade. I don't feel as though I am running a temperature, but during the night I opened my sleeping bag for extra cover and it felt good. I took my Mefloquine this morning with a multi-vitamin and a Sudafed/Tylenol number. About mid-morning I started to feel better but am still tired. I have to go to the sick bay for half an hour then back here for language.

Day XLV

Friday, May 31, 1996

Today I was supposed to go on another field trip but stayed here and slept, mostly. I have been running a low-grade temperature, occasional muscle and joint pain, headache, nausea, intestinal griping but no real diarrhea. I am totally exhausted and tired of it!

Crosby brought me my traveling money, along with some mail. I received three letters. One each from Maggie, Helen J. and Jim C. I answered Maggie's letter and improvised a birthday card for Bear. I put a piece of stale gum I had been carrying around since I left Ohio into the envelope with the card. On the outside of the envelope I wrote a message that the card contained gum, no money. It would be sad if the poor child didn't even get stale gum from his granny for his birthday. Not much of a present but I'm sure he'll get many gifts from others. With luck it'll arrive in time for his birthday.

I still haven't heard from Katie or any of her crew. I wonder if she is waiting to hear from me. In that case it'll be August before I hear. The latest postmark on letters has been May 10. Richard will not have received my letter from Lilongwe by that date. The mail should be getting through by now though.

I thought I would wait until I get to Lilongwe before I write more letters. I have been using the paper from this book for letters since I used up all the plain paper I brought to the village. When I get to Kasungu I can get airmail envelopes at the post office. Also perhaps I'll be able to get another notebook. I'll have this used up before I finish training at the rate I'm going. I should have time for writing as I understand there is electricity. However, I'm a bit skeptical about what I hear after the cold showers at camp!

Hey, don't complain, Granny. You are in the Peace Corps or soon will be! You volunteered for this and it isn't as bad as you

142

expected. You know things are better for you than they were for the first volunteers thirty-five years ago. You're soft! Admit it!

Day XLVI

Saturday, June 1, 1996

I feel better today. Not a lot, but somewhat. Whatever I have, I think my immune system is finally kicking in. I just don't know how my body could even think of getting sick with all the immunizations and antibodies that have been pumped into it! But I guess it did. I only wish I had some energy!

Day XLVII

Sunday, June 2, 1996

I woke up at the usual time, was bathed, etc., by seven thirty. I think I'm finally over this wretched whatever. I hope anyway. I haven't been doing much and yesterday was better than Friday. The game plan for today and the next several days should be exciting. The Peace Corps van will be taking us to Kasungu. Everyone is to be visiting their assignment posts. For Karlene, Robert and me, that is Kasungu. Therefore, we will stay there. Robert is with the Agriculture Department; Karlene and I will go to the District Hospital. Karlene as an AIDS co-ordinator and me as a child survival officer. We will be staying with Rob, Karlene's counterpart. I am packed except for the things I will tie up in my chitenji.

Alison, the van driver, took a group of us to the bus station in Kasungu. I am having increasing difficulty getting into the back of the van. By putting the backpack and chitenji in first, I still need to work hard to lift myself into the thing. It is embarrassing. I have the feeling I may fall or go flat on my face! Oh, well; I got in and nothing happened!

We waited at the bus station until the traveling group and their gear were settled; then Alison took Karlene and me to the District Hospital to find Rob. Rob was not there. Alison, a knowledgeable person, knew where Rob lived and took us to Rob's home. This is exciting, as Karlene and I were going to see where we would be living. We are to live in Rob's house when he leaves in July. The house is quite a drive from the hospital. When we got to his house, Rob wasn't there. Karlene left a note telling Rob we would be at the Kasungu Inn. Apparently, no one told Rob he was having guests for a couple of days!

The house, what we could see of it, is nice, brick, surrounded by a high brick wall with those same shards of glass I found so dismaying in Lilongwe. There is a metal grill gate in the front. This is where Karlene left the note.

The ever-protective Alison brought us to the Kasungu Inn and I booked a room. Karlene wanted to wait, for several reasons, but she had the option of registering later. We parked our gear in the room and walked back to the center of town, or whatever. We walked down the main street.

There we found a restaurant, the Golden Dish, where we had dinner. Not lunch but dinner. That was the only meal I'd eaten today. No. That statement was a lie. I had bread and tea this morning in the village, although it seems as though it was eons ago, in another life.

From the restaurant we walked to the bus station, then back to the hospital. We left Rob another note telling him we were at the Kasungu Inn. Then we walked back here (the inn).

I did my laundry in cold water. No water at all comes from the hot water tap and the cold water never stops running. I was going to wash my clothes yesterday and didn't for a couple of reasons. One was that Agnes was getting her things ready as she was leaving for school and two, I didn't feel like it.

I'm bummed out at this point. Karlene is taking a nap, or trying to, my socks are dripping water on the floor and I am sitting in a chair by a window, thinking.

I need to sort out what is happening. My resolve is wavering. I'm not sure if this just happened, or the fact that I didn't feel great last week may have something to do with it. I'm not as bothered by it now as I was earlier, but I am doing some motive reassessing. I've been on this route before but I felt good then. I knew I might get sick while here. However, thinking about being sick and actually being sick are two different things. Besides, I'm not really "sick" sick, I just feel rotten. It is affecting my thought processes and my ability to make rational decisions.

First, why did I decide to join the Peace Corps? Why did I not back out when it would have been less complicated than wait until now? What will I do if I go back? What do I really want to do about this?

A. Reasons why I joined the Peace Corps:

1. Something I have wanted to do for a long time.

2. Am able to volunteer my time without a large financial outlay.

3. A way of traveling to places I wouldn't or couldn't otherwise.

4. Can use my abilities in ways I might not be able to elsewhere.

B. Can I do the same thing or something similar some other way? Probably.

C. Physically is this more demanding than I expected or am able to tolerate? Possibly.

D. Am I unhappy? No.

E. What are my concerns?

1. Hauling heavy gear long distances.

2. I feel totally out of control.

3. I am wondering what would have happened today if Alison, the P.C. van driver, hadn't waited around to be sure we were okay? He did, so it isn't a concern.

4. The next time he might not be available.

5. Traveling long distances on a bus with a backpack I can hardly lift plus a bulky sleeping bag doesn't seem like a good idea.

F. I think I had best rethink what I want to do here.

1. I have already arranged my life so I can do this for two years. What will be the end result if I change course?

2. I am committed to what the Peace Corps does and stands for.

G. Ambivalence.

1. I don't want to give up.

2. I feel as though physically I may not be able to handle the job.

3. I don't need to make a decision now.

4. I'll check things out tomorrow.
5. Perhaps I'll feel better tomorrow.

Rob and Stephanie showed up at around three o'clock. I had met Stephanie at the camp's lodge party. She is a horticulturist and works at the park part time. Rob I haven't met before. Here we have the Bobbsie twins, all grown up. They looked as though they belonged together; a set as it were. They visited for a while and left.

After they left, Karlene and I decided to walk to the P.T.C. store to get some junk food for our supper. Whom should we meet again but Stephanie and Rob. They had gone to the Golden Dish for a drink and came out at about the time we finished browsing around the P.T.C. They walked back to the Kasungu Inn with us, then went on their way. Karlene found something to occupy herself with; here I sit, feet propped up, absolutely exhausted. Again!

Day XLVIII

Monday, June 3, 1996

I woke up around five o'clock and took a cold sponge bath. I don't think I want to deal with anymore cold showers. I did wet my hair, washed it, then rinsed it under the shower. That was as far as my stamina went.

I ate breakfast in the dining room here. I had bread, cereal, milk and a little margarine on the bread. I also had tea.

Karlene and I walked to the hospital to meet with Rob. We arrived around seven thirty and he wasn't there yet. The matron in charge was getting night report. Since there wasn't much use in standing around and we wanted to explore our future city, we started walking again. Our first stop was the post office. This, a short distance from the hospital. I was able to mail the letter I wrote to Maggie and Bear's card. Rob still wasn't there when we returned ten minutes later. Karlene mentioned that Robert was leaving his key and we could put our bags in his room and retrieve them this afternoon. That way we wouldn't need to worry about getting them out of our room by ten o'clock.

So we walked back to the inn, got Robert's key, put our bags in his room and turned the key to our room in at the desk. I had paid for the room before we left the first time.

With that out of the way, we went back to the hospital. This time, Rob was there and we were shown the way to his office. His office was in another building in the rear of the one we entered with the center main entrance. The hospital appeared to be a series of several, single-level buildings connected by walkways.

Rob explained he could show us around; however, the proper protocol was to go through the matron. The matron, it appears, was on bereavement leave. Her son had recently been killed in a motorcycle accident. Now we must go through her assistant. We remained in his office talking to him until he felt she was free.

Then he showed us to her office where we presented our letters of introduction. The assistant matron was Mrs. Chipeta.

She was the nurse who had shown us around last week on our tour of the hospital. She gave us some demographic information, talked to us for a while, then took us to meet the D.H.O. or district health officer, Dr. Ratsma.

Dr. Ratsma was gracious to us but explained to me she didn't want or need a child survival officer. What she wanted was someone to start a home-based care project for terminally ill AIDS patients. She was not happy that her precious resources and space at the hospital were being used for patients who couldn't be helped. She has a one hundred and sixty bed facility that at times will fill to three or four hundred patients. This happens, especially during the rainy season when there are epidemics of malaria and diarrhea. By setting up a program to teach families to care for the patients properly at home, the patients will have the advantage of being at home with their families and the hospital's limited resources can be directed towards patients who can be helped. She was anxious to get started on this. She had colleagues in the south who had started such a program and it was working well.

This sounded like something I would love to sink my teeth into. At this point I saw two problems. One, I would need to find out from the Peace Corps' Malawian office if I would be allowed to do this. And two, I was not sure I could physically handle it. I would return to Mphoma, talk to my superiors and think about this. I would let her know the decision by the end of the week.

After our interview with Dr. Ratsma, Mrs. Chipeta gave us a tour of the hospital. It was primitive by U.S. standards. However, the people all seemed knowledgeable, well trained and were functioning as well as possible under the circumstances. All of the departments we visited today were busy and had large numbers of patients. Everyone was gracious and polite. We went through several clinics, the kitchen, the laundry, the laboratory and various wards. We were finished around eleven thirty and I am totally exhausted again.

Karlene and I went to the Golden Dish for dinner again. I ate rice and chicken and drank two Cokes. I was full but no less exhausted.

I decided to spend one more night in Kasungu and go back to the village in the morning. Back at the inn, I asked if they had rooms with hot water. I knew they did as Robert had a room with hot water. Yes, they did; my new room has hot water! Yea! I retrieved my bags from Robert's room and transferred them to my room. I had nothing important that needed to be done. I washed my underwear and the pink golf shirt. I decided to pass on the denim skirt. It looked as though I had either slept in it or rolled it in a ball. Actually, I did have it rolled to pack it. Those wrinkles hung out. It was the wrinkles made from wringing out the water that needed the help of an iron. The iron I brought was in Lilongwe with everything else. Had I known how easy the other skirts were to care for and how functional, I would have left the denim there too. I like the denim as it has pockets and also I don't need a slip when I wear it. The slips though are as easy to care for as the skirts.

I was utterly wilted so just rested. It feels good not to have to push myself and just sit. While awake, I studied. I have many handouts to study. These are loaded with information that is important to know. So, I passed the time. I had no energy to do otherwise.

Day XLIX

Tuesday, June 4, 1996

I was awake at five o'clock. A warm shower was delightful. Then I washed my underwear, hung it up to dry and got dressed. It is amazing how quickly some of the things dry.

At seven Karlene walked with me to the bus station. The man informed me I had just missed a bus. There would be another between eight and nine. Back to the inn. I had breakfast with Karlene, Robert and Robert's supervisor. After breakfast, Karlene walked with me back to the bus station then left me as she had to spend time with Rob. She will be replacing him and he is to show her what he has been doing. At this point I am in no man's land. I have no position.

Standing in the bus station was an education. There was no one in the ticket office. I posted myself near the window so that when someone appeared I could ask him for a ticket to Mphoma village. When someone finally did come to the window, a mob of people surrounded the window to buy tickets. After the crowd was taken care of, I went to the window and told him where I wanted to go. I had to wait until the bus arrived before he would sell me a ticket. One would be coming. I waited. I had my backpack on the floor by a wall where I could watch for buses and was sort of guarding the wall. Not holding it up, but close.

As I stood there, people came and people went. Several would stand near for a while, people alone, people with families, moving slowly with no apparent purpose. A moving, liquid mass, with no way I could determine how the system functioned. I just determined I would go up every time a bus came until the right one arrived. There were no announcements and I probably would not have understood if there had been. Occasionally, the ticket man would appear, people would materialize from wherever, mob the window, get their tickets and board a waiting bus. When I ventured again to the window to ask about my bus, it was, "Not yet." I'm glad he spoke a little English. Had he replied, "Dakrani pongono," I would have died. Not really. That was a desperate statement but I was sure I would be standing there for days before anyone missed me.

Then a larger crowd began to gather. There were a large number of teenagers of both sexes starting to congregate. One young man who appeared to be fifteen or sixteen asked me in excellent English if I was in the Peace Corps. I have the only white face in the whole bus station so it was a good guess. I was thrilled someone could understand me. I explained where I was going and that I wasn't sure what bus I was to get on. That was no problem. He was going back to school in Mzuzu and I would be taking the same bus he was. We talked for a while and, sure enough, here came our bus and the largest crowd yet! I gave the young man 20K and told him I would watch his bag if he would buy me a ticket. The dear young man agreed and got in line. I don't think at this time I could handle the pushing and shoving in line. It was a particularly pushy-shovey crowd. A guard with a nightstick came from somewhere to encourage the ticket purchasers to stay in a reasonable line and not push up to the line out of turn. None of the other buses needed a nightstick... What am I getting into?

Eventually my knight in shining armor came over to me and handed me a piece of paper. Would this get me on the bus? Well, I'll try. I picked up my backpack and chitenji, wrapped sleeping bag, etc., and followed the crowd to the bus.

The bus boarders were acting the way they did at the ticket window, trying to stuff themselves into the bus. I couldn't do this. I got fairly close to the door, holding my piece of paper. There was no way I was going to fit on this bus! I have been on crowded buses in my life but this was unreal... Then another hero with a nightstick helped clear a space by the bus step and told me to get on. There was someone on the step and I told the nightstick there was no room. He said, "There will be." Sure enough, about five or six people came struggling through the crowd on the bus and got off. Then there was a little room, so I went up the steps into the bus. The driver took my backpack and sleeping bag and threw them behind him on a pile of bags. I am being crushed by the people getting on. I have my left foot on the floor, actually, the toe on the floor with my leg at some skewed angle. I'm leaning over the engine, with my right hip against that and my right leg down there somewhere. I am trying to hold myself in an upright position, with my right hand on the engine hood and no place to put my left arm except to hold it tightly against my body. The driver and the conductor had the space on the other side of the engine hood. I was being pushed that way by the crowd on the left. There was a sign over the windshield that announced, "Capacity 23". I didn't want to say anything, but there were that many bodies between me and the door. I was up in front!

They were mostly young people; I suppose on their way to Mzuzu to school, as was my young friend. He was farther back than me. I don't know how he got back there as he was behind me in the line. Actually, I do know. I was pushed to the spot where I ended up because while I watched my bags get stowed, the rest were moving in behind me and held me in position.

I was not comfortable. I complained about the seats on the Peace Corps bus? Ha! Malawians are small; I am not. The seats are fine for them. I'll never complain again! This wasn't even a seat.

My right foot was starting to fall asleep and the bus hadn't even started. When everyone was on the bus, with much grinding of gears we started off. I was able to see down the gear shift into the mechanism, so riveted my attention on that. The bus moved slowly away from the station, onto the street, through the market which was close to the bus station, and on to the main street. Here the driver had to make a safety stop. With more grinding of gears, the bus lurched forward into a left turn and toward M-1. At M-1 he made a right turn. More grinding of gears and as the bus gained speed, to be shifted into a higher gear, the gears wanted to rebel. They did not want to go faster. Either that, or the clutch wouldn't let them. The driver was struggling. He got moving. It seemed fast, but I don't think it was 50 kph; 50 kph is not fast and my leg is calling "Help!" Too bad down there. We are in this together.

Soon the bus starts making stops and letting people and

luggage off at the roadside. The crowd shifts a bit with each stop and, after a few such stops, I am able to move my leg a little; not necessarily into a more comfortable position. I'm now beginning to hope I recognize the Nyasulus' house when we pass it or I may end up in Mzuzu too!

By the time we pass the Nyasulus' house, I tell the driver I want off, and he stops the bus; it is quite a distance beyond the intersection by the store/market. My bags are unceremoniously thrown to the side of the road, and I step down from the bus after them. Ha! I almost fell on my face! My leg, the squashed one, the complaining one, was not going to allow me to go unpunished! However, after a mild rebellion, it did its proper duty as a good leg should, and I was able to maintain my balance, albeit, not gracefully! I'm sure the locals, to whom the mazungus were a never-ending source of amusement and wonder, were thinking, "Look at the old one! She's drunk! Let's watch her walk!" There were then more complaints from the legs when I bent to pick up the backpack and shoulder it. They came through again. The sleeping bag in the chitenji was easier.

One of the technical trainers was at the store across the road from the market: the one with the pump for its well. He was just leaving on his bicycle and was surprised to see me. Not so surprised that he forgot to be courteous, however. He asked if he could take one of my burdens on his bicycle. I gratefully thanked him and gave him the chitenji. He pedaled away towards the Nyasulus' as I trudged slowly behind.

I wasn't supposed to be back until Thursday but nothing the old mazungu lady did surprised anyone. The Nyasulus welcomed me with aplomb. I was so glad to be back, I wanted to hug Mayi but we don't do those things. I just told her I was glad to be back.

I am exhausted again but felt I must tell the authorities of my adventure. I walked to the sick bay and discussed things with Rose. Rose was non-committal and said I must wait until Friday when Edith arrived. Edith has the final say about everything. Wait I must.

Joyce is sick and Rose is caring for her at the sick bay. Rose and I talked outside so as not to disturb Joyce. Joyce is such a kind person; it is sad she is not feeling well. She is in good hands with

Rose caring for her. I think she must be the first patient at the sick bay.

My fatigue continues. I took a nap after I talked with Rose. Then I was in bed by seven.

Day L

Wednesday, June 5, 1996

I woke up about six with a nasty headache. I was in bed early and fell into a sound sleep. I remember hearing the clock strike several times during the night but didn't really get up until I woke up with the headache. I don't think it was hurting during the night; I wouldn't have slept so well. I took a Sudafed with Tylenol. I'm glad I brought them with me. They have usually helped the headaches I have had. I would sometimes get a "stuffy" nose which was the reason I brought them. The allergy symptoms haven't seemed to bother me here but the 500 mg of Tylenol seems to take care of the headaches. It did this time and I felt better after about half an hour.

I had my tea and bread while I sat on my bed this morning. I don't usually do this but am trying to get a couple of letters finished to mail. I wrote one to Mary, one to Jim and one to Helen. I am going to wait a few days to mail Jim's as I want Mary's to have a head start. She might not be happy if he gets a letter from me before she does.

At about eight I walked to the sick bay to see if Chris or Crosby were there so I could give them the letters to mail. There was no one at the sick bay, which surprised me. I started along the path to Chris's home when who should I meet but Rose and Joyce. Joyce looked as though she was not feeling fit. They had been to one of the homes so Joyce could bathe and were on their way back to the sick bay. They told me Chris was at "home". I continued on to his place.

Sure enough, I found Chris sitting on a bench with one of his family members shelling peanuts. Judging by the number in the container, they had been at it for a while or were fast shellers.

I gave Chris the letters. He told me he would be going to Kasungu later and would mail them. He asked me how my visit to Kasungu had gone. I told him what Dr. Ratsma had said and what she wanted, etc. He also was non-committal but gave me encouraging words. After talking with Chris for a bit, I headed back towards the sick bay. When I reached the sick bay. Rose was outside. She was on her way to get some tea for Joyce. We chatted for a while. Then who should come driving up but Dr. Ratsma in her four-wheel-drive hospital vehicle. She had her car full of people and equipment. She stopped the car, got out and talked with us. She told me she had my letter of introduction written. If I decide to do this, when I go to Mulanji on Saturday, I should stop and get it to deliver to her friends in Mulanji.

I explained I must talk to Edith before I could do anything. Edith is not expected before Friday and it would be then before I know. I would love to try this. I just hope Edith thinks it is a good plan, but I didn't tell Dr. Ratsma that. She then got back into her car and went on down the road. I guess today is clinic day.

I said goodbye to Rose and came back here. Mayi gave me some corn to shell. I sat in the backyard and did that. It is a pleasant task, doesn't take a lot of energy and I am resting my burning eyes.

A couple of weeks ago I was watching the copulating chicken and asked Carol if the hens sat on eggs at this time of year. In the northern hemisphere this is the time of year for "setting" hens and little chicks. Since here it is winter, even though it is warm, I thought perhaps that sort of thing went on in November and December. Carol, not having been raised on a farm, wasn't sure. Well, it seems these are northern hemisphere chickens as about three momma hens are parading around the yard now with rather large broods of chicks. The chicken are shining black and the chicks are dark fuzz balls. The backyard is full of interesting activity.

I came in out of the sun around ten thirty as it was getting too warm for me. I wasn't tired but the sun was hot. I didn't want to read or write because of my eyes. I am almost out of Hypotears. I am using them so much. I should have brought three bottles. Normally, one bottle lasts longer than a couple of months and I thought two bottles would be plenty. I didn't need them at all until I arrived in the village and even then not until I had been here a while. Then, it was eye wash time! Perhaps if I had been using them right along it wouldn't have happened? But I didn't and it did. I'll never know for sure and I don't intend to waste time worrying about it.

There are Visene drops in the medical kit but they don't help dry eyes. They are okay for red eyes as they constrict the blood vessels but they also dry the eye surface. This I don't want. These should last until I get to Mulanji. Perhaps Mary C. will be able to direct me to a pharmacy where I can get some lubricating drops. If worst comes to worse, I suppose I could get someone to boil me some water and make my own saline solution to use. Or I could ask Lucy if they have some normal saline I could use. Meanwhile, "let go" of it. I still have a little left in the bottle. I have a couple of bottles with my other stuff but I won't be reunited with that until I am assigned somewhere.

I have been thinking about the events of the last few days and am more certain than ever that God is looking after me. This has been a real opportunity to tune "inside" and I am comfortable. What happens will happen. I can't, however, allow myself to get excited of doing this project in Kasungu. It is hard not to. I don't have my group, but my "family" here, the Nyasulus, the trainers, the trainees are and have been helpful, kind and supportive.

Day LI

Thursday, June 6, 1996

Today the trainees should be returning. It has been strange being the only one of the group here; no classes, etc. For me it is probably just as well. I haven't been reading but have been writing letters and here in my journal. Using my eyes while writing doesn't seem to bother them as much as the reading.

It started out cloudy and a little cool, but turned into another sunny warm day. Mayi told me that Lucy, Sabina and Edith came from Lilongwe yesterday. Lucy stays next door with Bambo's nephew's widow. Sabina may stay there also but I'm not sure of that. I thought perhaps I would be able to talk to Edith today; then I wouldn't need to wait until tomorrow.

I walked to the sick bay to see if Edith was where I could talk to her and also to find if any of the others had returned yet. No on both counts. Edith did not come. Only Lucy and Sabina. Perhaps Mayi had Edith mixed up with Siti. Siti is the head of the nursing school at the University of Lilongwe. She conducted some of our technical training classes. Edith is the head of the Peace Corps technical training classes and assignments. I talked to Siti, Rose and Anna for a while. They were encouraging but unable to tell me I could or could not do this thing. That was Edith's jurisdiction.

I also found that most of the trainees were still away. Apparently, only one of the fellows returned and they weren't sure which one. I went back to the Nyasulus' and hung out.

I wrote some letters, shelled corn, watched Agnes make nsima, took a nap, etc. Agnes let me stir the nsima after it had been cooking for a while. I mean she allowed me to "try" to stir the nsima. That's what I did; try. Nsima is very thick. I watched while Agnes continued to add ofa to the boiling water, stirring continuously until it was the proper consistency. Then she suggested I try stirring. It was a joke of course. I could hardly move the spoon through the stuff! My muscle strength has deserted me!

I have tried to increase my muscle strength by exercising them. That only aggravates and makes it worse. I feel good today. Other than not being able to stir nsima, I'm okay. This fatigue and muscle weakness concerns me. I won't be able to do this job. Being a Peace Corps volunteer requires at least a moderate amount of physical strength and for some reason, mine is gone, or much of it. When getting into the back of the van is a major effort there is a problem. I can't put my finger on anything physical and I can't believe I aged that fast! Besides, even ninety-year-olds can increase their muscle strength by exercise and I'm not sixty-five yet.

Day LIV

Sunday, June 9, 1996

I skipped a few days here. Most of the trainees had returned by Friday and there was a farewell dinner at the sick bay. I didn't much feel like going but it was a command performance. I went. I sat through the speeches and ceremonies. When they started serving food I told Mayi I was going back to lie down, which I did. She was concerned and apparently left a short time after I did.

I went to bed and fell asleep. I woke up sometime during the night having chills and stomach cramps. I opened my sleeping bag which felt good as an extra cover. But I didn't go back to sleep and was miserable. I felt as though I should make a trip to the chim and felt too lousy to do that. I forced myself to go out there and wondered the whole time if I would make it back. Yes, it was diarrhea but that wasn't the worst of it. Along with the chills, my heart started racing and the beat as highly irregular. I thought the diarrhea, although it was only one stool, had lowered my potassium level. Perhaps I should try the electrolyte replacement that was in the medical kit. I opened the kit and, in the search for the electrolytes, found the thermometer. I decided to take my temperature.

I poured a packet of the mix into my drinking water, shook it up and started to drink it. It was awful! It was worse than drinking salt water but I did drink it. The irregularity stopped or lessened as did the rapid heart rate. I don't know if the salts helped or if things just straightened out on their own.

My temperature was 102.6°. I never have a temperature that high; 99.4 is the highest it has been in years. It would get up to 100 when I would get tonsillitis when I was young; never since I had my tonsils out. But this is beside the point. I felt awful. Making and drinking the salt water and taking my temperature was an effort. And no way was I going back to the chim. I would rather hold it. Oddly, the pressure went away.

That night was a week long. By morning I felt better. I had to get up. I had to get ready to go to Mulanji, so got up, went to the chim, more diarrhea, took a bath, got dressed, everything packed and ready for the van to take me to Kasungu to get on the bus. Everything was such an effort and I was close to tears. When the van stopped, I went out and told Chris I wasn't able to go. I just wanted to stay here and sleep. He told me I would need to arrange it with Lucy. I did let loose with the tears when they left without me and again when I got to Lucy's. She took my temperature, blood pressure and other vitals. Everything was normal. She then told me I would go to Lilongwe with them later.

I went back to the Nyasulus', lay down on the bare mattress in my clothes and fell asleep. I mostly slept all day, making a few trips to the chim.

At some point the van came to take me to Lilongwe. All the trainers and their gear were piled in the back. Adam, who, I discovered, had also put in a bad night, was in the front seat with the driver. With much effort, I was in the seat beside him with my backpack, sleeping bag and the little basket Mayi had given me "to take to the market". We were off to Lilongwe.

We hadn't been traveling long when I had to "go" again. I held it during the night and could do it again. I was too much into my misery to enjoy the ride. When we finally did get to Lilongwe, the driver had to take the trainers home. We made several stops to let the trainers out. After being in the village, it seemed strange to see normal-type homes similar to those one might see in any suburb.

The driver took me to a guest house called "The Ivy". The place was full but they gave me a room that may have been a family member's. There were no other guests that I could see. I had to take my shoes off and leave them by the door. Then was led by an attractive, young oriental woman to a room. It was small, with a bed and a chair, pegs to hang things on and it was clean. We entered a door in one end of the narrow room, I placed my backpack and sleeping bag on the chair, and the young woman led me through another door at the opposite end. This door led into a room with a sink and refrigerator. There were four doors that opened into this room. Three of them were bedrooms, one mine, and the fourth was the restroom with washbasin, shower and toilet. The young woman, whose name was Clara, opened the refrigerator and pointed out bottled water for drinking. No tap water, please.

I was glad to have a toilet so close! As soon as Clara left me, I used it. The first of many trips throughout the night. I then put on my nightshirt and went to bed.

That brings me to this morning, Sunday. I haven't had anything to eat since Friday, lunch, I think. I think I ate lunch on Friday, but I can't remember eating it if I did. Friday's activities are a little sketchy in my mind. I mostly remember sitting through that endless program and wanting desperately to go to sleep.

At this moment I would love some Campbell's tomato soup and some saltines. I feel better this morning. That better is a relative thing. Better than what? Better than I felt yesterday morning? Yesterday morning seems a lifetime ago.

Last night I made up my mind. I'm going home. Home? I have no home. I'm Dorothy in Oz. I gave that up to come here. Now I'm going to give this up the first time I get sick? Right now I don't have the other trainees or my family in the village. All I have is my higher power and I think he is on vacation in Kansas.

Yesterday, Adam, who is also ill got to go to the Kalikuti. I had been there before. I knew what it was. I wanted to go to the Kalikuti too. Today I'm glad I'm here. This is better. It is brighter, cleaner, I have a window, a beautiful yard to look at from it and it has a shower with hot water.

I took a shower and got dressed. Clara knocked on the door and asked if I would like something to eat. She would bring me something to eat or I could go to the restaurant. The restaurant, she said, was only about twenty meters away. I opted to go to the restaurant. The walk, I felt would be good for me. I didn't walk. Clara took me in her car. The restaurant was closer to one hundred meters than twenty. I was glad for the ride.

When I walked into the restaurant who should be there but Sue, Suzanne, Christa, plus a Peace Corps volunteer whom I hadn't met before. Scott also was to join the group. Now I know why the place was full yesterday! The trainees had missed connections to their destinations, therefore had to spend the night in Lilongwe. It was good to see familiar faces!

I ate toast, jelly, cereal and had some tea. This tasted good but I shouldn't have eaten so much. I wasn't queasy when I finished, but uncomfortable. After I had finished breakfast and said goodbye to the others, I walked back to the guest house.

I had been given a key to get in, so I unlocked the door, stepped inside, removed my shoes and went into my room. It would probably be a good idea to wash my underwear. It seems to me I was going to do some laundry on Friday but felt so punk that I didn't. I can't really recall what all I did on Friday. I'm not sure, but I think we went to the sick bay and were given traveling money. I vaguely remember Jane and Vyrle being there for the meeting, or perhaps I'm hallucinating! I guess it doesn't matter but I think I decided to wait until I got to Mary C.'s in Mulanji to do it. I think I lost a couple of days here…

Well, I'm safe. At this point, no diarrhea, so perhaps I'll start feeling better. This mess has been dragging on and on. The depression scares me. This has just started. I don't know how I'm going to deal with that. I can keep my thoughts directed most of the time, but at times the tears just want to flow. I suppose it is just part of the fatigue.

I did wash my underwear and socks and hung them on the pegs to dry. I even washed the socks I was wearing and am sitting here barefoot.

Agnes had put a package in Mayi's basket sometime before I left yesterday. I didn't open it as I felt too rotten to care. I opened it this morning. It was a chitenji. I love it. It was a thoughtful thing for her to do. Now I have two. I thought, after I discovered how useful they were, I should have bought another when I bought the first. However, it was confusing at the time and a learning experience. A chitenji would have been one of my first purchases when I get settled. Now I have another.

We passed the Kasungu market several times but I never went into it. It was smaller than the one in Lilongwe and appeared a little neater. I still don't know if I'll be allowed to go to Kasungu. At this point, I don't care. Nothing seems important.

This afternoon I walked to the restaurant and ordered chicken soup and rice with vegetables. The chicken soup was just delicious. I put some of the rice mixture into the soup. By the time I finished the soup, I had eaten too much again. I brought the rice and vegetables back here with me and put them into the fridge.

Lucy came by this afternoon to check on me. She said they will come pick me up tomorrow and run some tests. Stool sample. By that time, there won't be anything left in me or I'll be constipated. It's still diarrhea, but lessening. Of course, now I am eating.

I sat here and ate cold rice and vegetables with my fingers! I don't believe I did that. It was delicious, even cold. What the heck! I like cold pizza; why wouldn't I like cold rice and veggies? And what's wrong with my fingers? I washed my hands well before and after I ate.

Day LV

Monday, June 10, 1996

It is almost eleven thirty and I have just returned from the Peace Corps headquarters. Adam knocked on my door nearly as soon as I returned from the restaurant and announced that a driver was here to take us to see Neni. He had been on antibiotics and felt well enough to travel. Mike was at the P.C.H. already when we arrived. He was waiting for someone from the Forestry Department. Everyone was at a meeting. We cooled our heels until close to nine thirty.

Then everyone arrived; Jane, Vyrle, Rose, Sabina, Naomi and Edith. I was supposed to see Edith after talking to Lucy and Neni but she was in another meeting by then.

I was ushered into the medical office and met Neni. We discussed my symptoms and she asked for a stool specimen. I conveniently was able to provide one. She also gave me some orange Gatorade mix. She thought perhaps it would help. I took it. I have been drinking plenty of fluids and eating. The possible electrolyte imbalance I may have had was possibly resolved with the mess I drank Friday night–Saturday morning, whenever. That last sentence was "iffy"! My heart has not been going pat-pitty-pat-pat since that one episode. The racing along with the irregularity was unnerving. Usually the irregularity happens when I overdo the caffeine intake. Oh, well, the Gatorade will be a change from water.

There was a scale by Lucy's desk and I stepped on it. I weigh one hundred forty-three pounds! I haven't lost much weight. Here I thought I was on the verge of starvation! I have a long way to go! I feel wasted; probably the effects of the diarrhea. My blood pressure was 120/70; right out of the textbook. They probably think I am malingering. I wish I was.

I'll give this a few more days. I am exhausted at this point;

again or yet. All I want to do is lie down. In fact, I don't know why I am sitting here writing this. I could be resting. I hope they find something in that specimen they can kill so I can get on with my life. If it is a virus, they can't kill it and I'll have to wait for my body to put a stop to its shenanigans or it will kill me. This is a bum deal. I didn't expect this to happen. I figured I would more likely get knocked off in a M.V.A. (motor vehicle accident), but not this.

As it is, I am a total waste and this could go on and on. I have been increasingly worthless since the week in camp; I keep thinking it will get better. Some days I feel good. My muscle strength is not that it was when I came here. I can hardly lift that stupid backpack and that should be getting easier to carry, not harder. I'll worry about that later.

It is about six forty-five and I just came back from the restaurant. It was getting dark when I walked over there and was dark walking back here. I'm not comfortable walking outside here in the dark. I suppose it is because I'm not familiar with the area. I don't usually mind being out alone after dark, at home that is. But that isn't walking around; it is usually to or from the car. And I'm always aware of who and what is around me. I won't do that again...

The cook – I think she is Clara's mother – is a regular mother hen. I ordered the rice and veggies. She came out of the kitchen and asked if I didn't want something else. She doesn't speak much English but she does better at English than I do Chichewa or Korean! What I think she said was, "No want chicken soup?" I had the chicken soup also. The body language was irresistible; I would do irreparable harm to myself if I didn't eat the soup. I have never eaten such delicious chicken soup. Ever. I dipped the rice and veggies in the soup again. It cools the soup a little. I brought the rest of the rice back here with me. I'll have it for breakfast.

Most of the afternoon was spent reading. I'm using the Visene now. It burns when I put them in but after the initial shock they feel better. I suppose anything would feel better after that burning! I have to limit the use of the Visene too but for now I'll live with it.

168

Day LVI

Tuesday, June 11, 1996

It is at this point nine twenty and I am sitting on my bed in The Ivy, bone weary. I woke up at six o'clock, brushed my teeth and used the last of the toothpaste. That is not as bad as using the last of the eye drops as I can always use soap. It tastes terrible and doesn't do a good job, however is better than nothing. I didn't take a shower right away this morning. There was no hot water. I did eat last night's leftovers. Then washed my dish and fork. Today I'll make it a point to go over at lunchtime for food. I don't want to go out again after dark.

The other Peace Corps people seem to stay hidden as there is never anyone around when I go to the restaurant. Only the first morning. They are all at the other end of the building. Not far, but isolating. Most of them probably feel as rotten as I do. I met several of them at the medical office. One had been bitten by a dog and needed two more rabies shots. I suppose they are as steeped in their misery as I am.

The people who run this building are kind but I am not easy to communicate with. My language skills are zilch and, other than Clara, they don't speak much English.

I keep wiping the pen tip off on a tissue to see if it will stop the blobbing. It works for a bit, but starts again. These pens don't seem to be great for the long haul. I brought along a box of Papermates I had purchased at Office Max for some paltry sum. I always liked the fine point for charting. But charting is different than the amount of writing I have been doing. I had packed two of the Papermates and my trusty old Parker when I left for the village. The Papermates were okay for a time but then started blobbing as I write. They have been a nuisance for the past couple of weeks. They are probably close to dying. I use the Parker sometimes but am afraid it too will run out of ink. I have refills in

169

my other bags but that doesn't help me here. I also have more Papermates in the other bags… I write and wipe and hope the ink continues to flow.

Writing here is like talking to myself. There is not much else to do. All I think about is how miserable I am. I'm tired and my eyes feel funny from the Visene. I can't use them more than four to six times a day and I want to flush!

I did decide to take a walk after I took a shower. I'm glad I did but it did a number on me. A walk! Here everyone walks. I love it. The sidewalks are jammed. I started making a map so I could find my way back. In the process, I discovered this street, Tsiranna Ave. It is parallel to M-1 and M-1 is not far from here. Because of all the stops that were made the day I came, and my state of mind, I had the impression that M-1 was miles from here.

There is a police station at the corner of Kasungu Procession Road and M-1, a traffic circle that adds confusion and a cinema. The cinema is across the road from the police station.

I walked along Kasungu Procession Road, crossed M-1 and continued until I came to what appeared to be a wholesale district. I walked over a bridge that spanned a river of sorts; this before I came to the wholesale district.

I'm getting weary by this time and retrace my steps back to The Ivy. I think I'll try again later this afternoon, after I eat. I'll try a different route. There must different paths through streets that run parallel to the Kasungu Procession Road, and I'll be able to cross M-1 away from the traffic circle. I'll try walking along the street the Korean Gardens is on to see if it crosses M-1.

It is now about eleven thirty and I have rested, dozed, perhaps even slept. Clara's mother came in and told me a lady in a car had come to see me. Then she said something else that made me think she was asking me if she came…

Lucy had dropped in while I was out. She was sending a driver for me sometime after one o'clock. She also told me nothing had showed up in the stool specimen. I suppose now they will want a blood sample. They could have done that yesterday. I was willing and waiting. But I'm okay. There is no hurry.

I think I'll tell them to make travel arrangements for me and I'll go back to the States. I can be sick there more easily than I can be sick here. I have been taking care of my own health, with God's help, for over forty-five years and never felt this out of control. God has been good to me and given me a healthy body. I don't see any reason to mistreat myself now. Who knows what else I'll be exposed to?

As much as I enjoyed the village, the Nyasulus and their wonderful family, I don't think the village stay needed to be that long. Bobbie was right when she said she didn't need it. She knew what the depression was like. It has been a wonderful opportunity to meet some great people such as the Nyasulus and a chance for them to meet some Americans. I'm afraid that, with me as an example, perhaps their impression wasn't as favorable as mine, however! But I'm wondering if the exposure to whatever was necessary.

The young people, some of them, had never been exposed to such deprivation. Perhaps knowing how hard living can be for some people will be helpful to them. Who knows? But there are different types of deprivation. Here it is material and physical. In the U.S. it is spiritual. I don't know which is worse. I guess I could stay here but if I continue to feel so weak, there is no way I will be able to accomplish anything useful. And, it is costing the U.S. taxpayers a lot of money to keep me here. The Malawian people don't need another ailing person here!

I'm feeling resentful and angry now that I'm sick and perhaps not being reasonable. I don't want to go back and give this up but I don't want to feel this way either. I'm absolutely out of control of anything here. Death I can handle. This is something else!

It is now five thirty and I do believe I'll forgo food tonight. I'm not hungry now and I don't want to go out in the dark. Clara just stuck her head in and wondered if I would like something to eat. I thanked her and said, "No."

I had walked to the restaurant at lunchtime. They weren't open for business but the family, I assume it was the family, was there having lunch. "Mother" was there and fed me too. Wonderful chicken soup and rice.

I came back here, brushed my teeth with "Giesha" soap and was sorry. Ughh! I have used soap to brush my teeth before but usually something similar to Ivory. I will never brush my teeth with perfumed soap again! The perfume lingers in the mouth longer than on the skin!

After that disaster, I sat on the front step and waited for the driver. He came by as scheduled and whisked me to the Peace Corps headquarters and Lucy. Blood pressure and vitals, normal. I told Lucy I had decided to go back to the states. Then I talked to both Neni and Lucy. Things were put into motion. I should leave here Thursday at six thirty in the evening and be in the States in seventy-two hours. I think that will be Sunday. If I am completely cured in the morning, I'll kick myself.

Neni informed me that what I am experiencing is normal for the Peace Corps volunteers as well as trainees and happened often. If I was having doubts, that took care of them. I can't see myself dragging around for the next two years! There are many viruses around and you just let your body heal. But what about the tears? Do they go away too? This really bothers me.

The paperwork has been started. I have my letter of resignation to Vyrle written, also a goodbye letter to everyone, and now I am writing this.

Tomorrow, Vyrle is going to bring, or have delivered, my luggage that has been stored at his place. I can sort through the stuff and jettison some of it. I certainly don't want to bother with it on the way back. Just the stuff in my backpack.

Day LVII

Wednesday, June 12, 1996

I spent a rather restless night. My adrenaline kicked in and I wouldn't know if I was tired or not. No diarrhea, No bowel movement period. I never thought I would become obsessed with bowel movements, but here I am, counting them! What is to become of me? Other than taking note of "no poop", my mind is working overtime. I wonder what the kids will think. That is a switch! I'm sixty plus years old. Who cares? I do, I guess. I hope this doesn't really matter to them. I think they were proud to have their mother in the Peace Corps. Then again, perhaps they join Kaye and some of my friends who think I was nuts... Well, I'll take this one day at a time and see that happens. No long-term goals at this point.

I flossed my teeth and brushed them with plain water. My mouth feels clean, if not refreshed. That Giesha soap was more than I needed this morning. The perfume lingers and lingers in the mouth. Too bad it doesn't on the skin. I wonder how I'll smell to people stateside? I said my adrenaline had kicked in. I'll probably sleep for a week if someone will give me a bed...

My bags should be getting here today, sometime. Then I'll have toothpaste! Hypotears! A clean nightshirt! Oh, yeah! Maybe I'll wear this one tonight, just for old times' sake. I won't need a nightshirt while traveling. When I get back, I'll be able to soak this one in Twenty Mule Team Borax and bleach. If there is anything left of it after that, perhaps it will be clean! Even my jacket has started taking on an essence of its own. Actually, it's mine. It's just weird. And, I'll have jeans! I'll wear those to travel! This day will wear me out! I can't leave for fear they'll come with my stuff! It's only eight thirty!

Well! How about that? My bags were delivered and I spent the morning sorting. "Mother" provided me with a box which I proceeded to fill. Guess what? I can't find toothpaste. I know it is there somewhere but can't find it.

I think I have my backpack down to a manageable weight but haven't tried to lift it. It is almost one o'clock, I'm exhausted, half hungry and sucking on a butterscotch candy. I can't decide if I should lie down or go get something to eat. I'm not sure whether the restaurant is open or not and there is no one around to ask. I don't feel like doing anything except rest. All that exertion and my adrenaline quit.

Guess what else? I discovered where the stain on my slip and panties came from. A leaking battery in the bottom of the backpack! I discovered it when I completely emptied the pack to shift stuff I wanted to carry with things I could put in the large bags. Knowing it came from a leaking battery doesn't make it look any better. At least, now I know where it came from.

I found a bulb in one of the bags. I had packed several and thought I would see if that was the problem with the big flashlight the Peace Corps gave me. After changing the bulb and three new batteries, the flashlight worked again. I put it with the stuff that was staying.

I got rid of many of the things I had brought. Someone will be able to use it. Now the large bags are not so heavy, nor is the backpack. I suppose if I felt more energetic, I could dig out some more but that is all for now.

I did decide a walk might be good for me. I don't know if it was or not. My energy level without the adrenaline is low, low. I started down the street the Garden is on. That does go to M-1 and there is a store there. I thought it was too late for the restaurant and figured I could get some junk food and toothpaste. I was almost at M-1 when who should come by but Clara. She offered me a ride as she thought I was going to the P.C.H. I told her, "No, thanks, I'm just taking a walk." She suggested I go back to the restaurant and get some chicken soup and some rice. I did the soup-rice bit and brought the leftovers back. "Mother" gave me a banana which I ate just because it was there.

I don't think walking to M-1 would have been such a great idea as I was totally exhausted by the time I returned here. I listened to tapes; Gershwin and Liszt. It is four thirty; too early to go to bed, although I feel as though I could. I guess I'll read for a while. I have been writing quite a bit since I have been here and have the time. I hope I don't run out of paper before I get home. I have been using the paper in this notebook for writing letters as I ran out of the other a long time ago. Oh! I have eye drops! Two more bottles in the bags!

Day LVIII

Thursday, June 13, 1996

This is the day I leave Malawi. I feel good this morning but who knows if I am better or my adrenaline is flowing again? Perhaps both. I walked to the restaurant for breakfast and just became a little breathless; so, perhaps it is going away. Or perhaps I was just suffering acute homesickness and will completely recover as soon as I get back to the States.

I am sitting here on my bed in my jeans and sweatshirt. Someone should be coming to pick me up and take me to headquarters. I should call to find out what is going on.

It was strange, using a telephone! The Chaos have a phone. I asked permission to call the P.C.H. and Clara helped me do so. I spoke with Paul who told me they would send a driver to pick me up at two o'clock.

I had been sitting in my room wearing a sweatshirt plus my jacket as I was chilly. Around one thirty I decided to move my bags on to the porch and wait in the sun. I sat in the sun and began to warm up. As I became warmer, I removed the jacket. After sitting for a while longer, I was warmer still. I then shed the sweatshirt. I had a golf shirt under the sweatshirt, therefore was not naked! The sun continued to warm my body. I moved to the side of the porch where there was a little shade. That was just right.

As I sat quietly, enjoying the pleasant surroundings, I happened to look at the ground near the base of the tree that was offering the shade. There stood the tiniest, iridescent blue bird I have ever seen. It was as small as or smaller than a humming bird. We looked at each other for what seemed a long moment, then he flew up into the tree and disappeared. I continued to sit quietly, hoping he would come back. He didn't. I was delighted I saw it at all!

The driver arrived at two o'clock, helped me load the luggage into the van and we were off to the P.C.H. My first stop was to see Lucy and Neni to receive my instructions. I am to continue to take the Mefloquine for four more weeks. When I get back I need to have an enzyme test, G6PD, to see if I can tolerate the Primoquine. The Primoquine I will need to take the last two weeks of the Mefloquine. This is to clear my liver of any cysts formed by malaria parasites that are resistant to the Mefloquine. I also will need to have stools checked for ova and parasites, twice. I hope I remember all that. I guess I don't have to; they have it all written out...

The second step was to see Paul. I had to give him all my kwatcha and I had a lot. I had the money I would have needed to travel to Mulanji and back, plus some that I didn't use in Kasungu. Then he gave me back my money, traveler's checks and credit card.

Third was Vyrle's office. That was Grand Central Station. I had to wait my turn. He was kind; probably used to people doing this. I gave him my letter of resignation and the letter of farewell to the trainers and trainees, my family for the past two months. That was sad; Chris called and I talked to him while I was still in Vyrle's office. Vyrle gave me my airplane tickets, passport, etc. Then on to see Betty where I received my travel itinerary.

After that it was waiting for the driver to take me to the airport. By this time, I'm exhausted again and it feels good to sit down. I do this in the lobby. While I'm there, Nancy and Danielle come in looking for a ride to the Kalikuti. This was the time the trainees were returning from their site visits. I talked to Jane and Sabina while I was waiting there and promised to mail a letter in the States for Jane.

Finally, the driver arrived to take me to the airport. He helped me with my bags and we started off. We weren't out of the parking lot when Bobbie came up to the van. She said, "I wish I could have talked to you before you decided to do this. That's the way it is in the Peace Corps. You sleep twelve hours a day and think you're depressed!" I lost it completely. This had been coming all week. Maybe if I had talked to her... I said with much difficulty, "I am depressed and can't handle it. Thanks anyway,

Bobbie, and God bless." I think the driver observed what was happening and quietly drove out of the parking lot.

The trip to the airport seemed to take forever. The driver spoke excellent English and we engaged in small talk. He was listening to a speech on the radio and explained a little of what was said.

By the time we arrived at the airport, I was completely drained. I did what I had to do. This was an international flight. They had to make sure I wasn't hauling contraband, etc. They could have stuffed my luggage with heroin. I wouldn't have known or cared for that matter. I went through the isolation booth, let the lady check my backpack, dealt with the baggage and boarding passes, etc. After I had taken care of all that and was free for a while, I visited the restroom. No bowel movement fortunately as there was no toilet paper nor soap to wash hands. Oh, well, I'm already sick...

The KLM people were friendly and kind. It got better after I boarded the plane. I was given an aisle seat. It was handy that I didn't need to climb over anyone to go to the restroom, but I don't ever want an aisle seat on a red-eye again. There is no place to place one's head except back, and I was so tired.

They served dinner soon after the take-off and I ate. I was hungry as I hadn't eaten anything since breakfast. The food was good but I was unable to eat much. We stopped in Nairobi where the plane filled up. We had flown through a storm and it was raining in Nairobi.

There was no one in seat A until we arrived in Nairobi, when a young French-speaking woman boarded. She didn't speak much English and my French is more dismal than my Chichewa so there wasn't much conversation. I didn't feel much in the mood for anything, let alone conversation. It was just as well we couldn't communicate.

I listened to tapes for a while after we left Nairobi. Later, the stewardess asked if I would like a headset as they were showing a movie. I said, "Yes." The movie was *Mr. Holland's Opus*. It was okay. Smaltsy but okay.

They served another meal on the flight but I turned that one down. I was still uncomfortable from the first meal. Breakfast was also served and I ate that not long before deplaning in Amsterdam.

Day LVIX

Friday, June 14, 1996

Sometime on that flight from Nairobi to Amsterdam, Thursday turned into Friday. It was daylight and the sun shining when I was able to see the ground from the window. I was in an aisle seat but on occasion the plane would tilt a little and I was able to see neat green fields. I assumed we were over Holland but couldn't be sure. The flight arrived in Amsterdam before seven. My bags were checked through so I just had the backpack to deal with. It wasn't loaded quite the way it was on the way over. My muscle strength was considerably lessened so it didn't seem any easier to carry.

The airport in Amsterdam, at least where I was, was bright, clean, airy appearing. The shops were there, the money kroners but I could use American dollars. I thought about buying souvenirs; think was all I did. It would be something more to carry. At this point, I had all I could handle. My flight to Detroit wasn't due to leave until ten forty-five. I had time to kill.

One of the first things I did was locate the ladies room. I am still having diarrhea stools. I found a seat near the ladies room as I knew I would be visiting it again. I did; several times. It is interesting as I didn't use the airplane facilities during the whole flight from Lilongwe to Amsterdam. I had to go as soon as I stood up and started walking. That was a twelve-hour flight. I lied a little. I emptied my bladder twice during the flight.

I sat down in the waiting area and waited. At first I was the only person there. As boarding time neared, the area filled up. They started the boarding process at nine fifteen. This was one full airplane. The row I was in had ten seats across. I was sitting in an aisle seat in the center section, row thirty-one. Also it seemed it was in the center of the plane. By multiplying ten times thirty-one, I calculated three hundred ten. Plus there were more rows behind the one I was in and another section beyond that. As the airplane narrows towards the back there won't be ten seats in a row; however, that is still a lot of passengers. As far as I could see, the plane was full.

As soon as we were in the air, I set my watch to coincide with the time in Detroit. I thought I was all set with the proper time. I have no conception of passing time as there was nothing to relate to. When I looked at my watch, it had stopped. I had neglected to push the stem all the way in when I changed time. I pushed the stem in and it started running. I had no idea how long it had been stopped. It could have been ten minutes or it could have been thirty.

The trip seemed endless. I felt rotten, was hot, couldn't get comfortable, my leg wanted to cramp, from sitting I imagine, and my "sit upon" was crying, "Enough! Get off me!" I made some trips to the restroom. I even went to different ones just to walk a bit. However, mostly I sat. I thought I would appreciate the return trip as it was more direct and had a shorter layover. However, it took its toll also.

The never-ending flight arrived in Detroit on schedule. The pilot announced the correct time as they always do. My watch had only stopped ten minutes. I reset it again and made sure the stem was all the way in.

Getting off the plane took forever. There were a zillion people on this flight. They were quietly multiplying during the flight and hiding under seats and in the overhead storage bins. After I shouldered my backpack and stepped into the aisle, it was take a step and wait, duck someone's bag falling from the overhead storage. My disposition was deteriorating rapidly. On a scale of one to ten, one being bitchy and ten merry sunshine, I started out somewhere around three or four and made it to minus six while deplaning.

My jaws are clenched, my muscles tensed and steam is issuing from my ears. My little wheels are spinning. I have fifty minutes to catch my commuter flight to Toledo X. The time seemed forever. Actually wasn't more than fifteen or twenty minutes before I arrived in the terminal. I was beginning to hope no one could pick me up and I could go to a Holiday Inn, Ramada or some such place, and sleep for three days.

But I had to do my thing here. With my legal papers in my hot fist, I stood in a rapidly moving line. As a citizen they didn't give me too hard a time going through that one. I thought, Why, this isn't so bad. If I don't have far to go to catch the commuter, I should make it easily. Ha!

Next I had to wait for the baggage carrousel to bring my large bags. Now I was becoming concerned I would never see them again. Finding them in that pile would be a miracle. There were several uniforms walking around with dogs sniffing luggage. One little beagle was more interested in sniffing some other things. Probably drugs in someone's purse or pocket. The uniform wanted him to sniff luggage and there was a war of wills going on while mountains of luggage were piling up. Some people were getting theirs while others were probably hung up in the immigration lines. There were several fellows taking the bags from the carrousel before they disappeared wherever they disappear to.

I was getting concerned I had missed mine or they were still in Lilongwe or Amsterdam. Finally! There they were! I suppose, since I started at the farthest point, my bags just ended up at the bottom as newer arrivals were piled on top of them. For some reason, they were among the last off. I managed to lift them from the carrousel and prayed I wouldn't need to haul them far.

The next stop was customs. Another wait. I didn't have anything to declare but still had to wait my turn. Once there I was through with the official business. The lady explained where I should take my bags so they would make the connecting flight; also where I needed to go to get the flight.

It wasn't that far. However, departure time had passed. When I arrived at the desk and showed the attendant my ticket, she looked at me and said, "Why did you miss it?" By this time I'm numb. The question irritated me and I wanted to scream, "Doesn't everyone miss planes on purpose? Why do you think I missed my plane, you bonehead!" But I didn't. I looked at her with my best evil eye, and said in a slow calm voice, "I was held up in customs." If I hadn't felt so crummy the whole thing would have been funny; but I wasn't feeling "ha–ha" funny.

The next flight would leave at four thirty. I could go on that.

Woody or someone was to have notified Richard I was coming home. My first project was to call Richard. They wanted three dollars. I had about two in change and had to buy a dollar fifty-eight cent can of Pepsi to get that. They were stingy with their change in that place. The second try was to call Richard and Katie collect. The operator would not allow me to talk to their machines as the machines might not pay for the call.

By this time I am so strung out, all I want to do is go to sleep. That is not to be. I sip the Pepsi and that gives me a lift. I sit down to watch the passing scene. People arrive, their planes arrive, they leave, more people show up and the merry-go-round continues. There I sit.

After about an hour, I try Katie again collect. This time she answers the phone. Fortunately for me, she chose that time to come into the house. They were all out in the pool. No, she didn't know I was coming home. Yes, she would call her siblings and let them know Granny was home and sick. Yes, she would pick me up at Toledo X at five o'clock.

I blow the rest of the change on another Pepsi and wait. There is a large tour group waiting for their plane. There are also several people who have been to Detroit for a golf tournament who are returning home. The area becomes quite busy. Around four twentyish, they announce my flight.

I pick up my backpack and truck out to the boarding area. What do you know? My little red devil is waiting for me! I surrender my backpack. I know the rules. Climb the steps, into the plane, fasten my seat belt. It is déjà vu.

Before five o'clock I deplane at Toledo X, claim my backpack and enter the terminal. I know my way around Toledo X, head for the baggage claim area, wait for the bags to come gliding up, haul them off the carrousel, wheel them to the front of the building and prepare to sit down on them. I look up and here comes Katie cruising to where I am. She stops the car, gets out and I am holding my daughter in my arms; the tears start to flow again. Not for long. She helps me load the gear into the trunk, we get into the car, fasten our seat belts and leave the airport. We stop at Mickie D's in Swanton. My first in two months!

Katie brought me home via Sean's baseball game in Hudson.

Ron, Melissa and Daniel showed up at Will Carlton Park before Sean's game was over. Ron had been with Melissa at her softball game and came to watch the end of Sean's game. Both teams won their games. Since Ron was there to bring Sean home, Katie and I left with Daniel and Melissa. I'm afraid I was being a real drag…

After we arrived at Katie's, Melissa and Daniel went swimming. I soaked my feet in bleach water, took a shower, put some Desenex between my toes, put on some clean socks and generally got ready for bed. I suspect I am going to throw away a pair of shoes!

Mary, Barry and Bear arrived around nine thirty or ten o'clock. It was so good to see them. I went to bed again not too long afterward, however. I wasn't able to sleep when I went to bed earlier. I had a cramp in my right hip and leg. Probably from the twenty-four-hour sitting marathon in airplanes. The Tylenol I had taken shortly before they arrived kicked in a short time after. I was able to sleep!

A Year Later: Summer 1997

Rewriting this journal has been a catharsis for me. Early in the summer I thought I had best get my act together and type it so it was readable. Only the most determined person can handle my penmanship. When it comes to grandchildren, the determination is more apt to be inclined towards not reading at all. This way I can give copies to friends and family who have expressed an interest in my Peace Corps experience; or rather lack of it. When I returned home, my physical and emotional state made it difficult to discuss more than generalities. For a time, when I returned home, I didn't want to see anyone or talk to anyone. My family was understanding and gave me the space I needed. Returning home was more difficult than going.

Rereading the journal was difficult for me as I relived much of the experience. As I rewrote passages to make them clearer to those who would be reading it, many of the feelings came back. Especially of the last weeks as I became increasingly weak and increasingly aware that there would be a problem if I stayed. The Peace Corps is not for the weak!

I never really made up my mind to return until I found out I was going to have to allow the disease to run its course. An intestinal infection was cleared up in short order with antibiotics. The weakness and depression have lessened but return at times. The depression only hits when I eat beans! From what I have experienced since returning, my time in Malawi would have been wasted; spent resting.

They haven't been able to find anything wrong with me. Age? Baloney! Even taking that into consideration, this is not part of the aging process.

Would I go back? In a heartbeat! If I thought I could function as a useful participant. I believe in the Peace Corps. I honestly feel that the most effective foreign aid money is that spent on the Peace Corps. The Peace Corps volunteers deal with people at a local level, using what is available and using their knowledge, help people help themselves. Starting projects that can be continued after the volunteers' departure.

The young men and women who were in training with me are indeed special. My village experience was easy compared to what the others dealt with; living with village families, learning first-hand what it is like to live in a situation that most of them could not imagine, and accepting it gracefully and with dignity. Gaining the awareness that a large percentage of the world's population don't have safe drinking water, adequate food, poor access to adequate or even minimum health care. It takes a strong, dedicated person to give two years of his or her life to helping those less fortunate.

We in this country have so much to be grateful for. Starting with the great abundance of food and resources that we take for granted. The chance to be educated that so many throw away. Our lack in this country is not material, it is spiritual. Fortunately, there are still a large number of people in this country who continue to remember what is important and live their lives accordingly.

Printed in the United States
61786LVS00001B/24